A Straightforward Guide
To
SAVINGS
AND
INVESTMENTS
LIVING WITH DEFLATION
AND RECESSION

2nd Edition

Anthony Vice

www.straightforwardco.co.uk

Straightforward Publishing
Brighton BN7 2SH

© Anthony Vice 2011

British Cataloguing in Publication data. A catalogue record is available for this book from the British Library.

ISBN 9781847162052

Printed in the United Kingdom by GN Digital Books

Cover Design by Bookworks, Islington London N1

Contents

INTRODUCTION

Chapter1. Check Your Bank   11

Chapter 2 . The protected investor   21

Chapter 3. Get plastic to help

INTRODUCTION

As everyone keeps telling us, life is going to be hard over the next year or so. The sad truth is that they are probably right.

Inflation is a problem, as China and other emerging countries compete for food and raw materials. In the UK, inflation is hitting at a time of low industrial growth and increased taxation. Jobs here are being cut, by government and private industry. One think tank reckons that households are now facing their worst financial squeeze since 1921.

In finance, the focus has completely changed. Only two to three years back, we were all concerned about safety. Would the High Street banks survive? If our own bank hit trouble, who would step in, and what would happen to the money we had put on deposit? Banks were rescued by governments right across the world, and compensation terms were greatly improved. Banks and building societies may still get into difficulties, but the typical depositor is much better protected.

Now, the key issue for all of us is whether we are getting the maximum benefit out of our financial resources. If life is going to be anywhere near has hard as the experts predict, we need to make the best use of our financial assets; above all, we need to protect income. We need to look again at our tax set-up, we need to make the best use of our credit cards and we need to keep down the cost of that holiday abroad. Rules change, sometimes in our favour sometimes not; it is important to keep up-to-date.

That does not mean that we have to retreat into some kind of financial bunker. Nor does it mean that we all have to turn into would-be financiers and spend our spare time pondering taxation and foreign exchange. But it does mean looking hard at all areas of individual finance and being ready to take action, probably one-off, with one clear objective: get income up, and/or get outgoings down.

Times are tough, but they will not last for ever, maybe even not more than a few years before recovery begins. One of the oldest fallacies in finance and politics is to believe that today's conditions will continue indefinitely, either the boom years of the earlier 2000s or the bank crisis of 2007-8. So think carefully before committing on the basis of today's values and be ready for the financial world to change - it frequently does, and it can move fast.

Whatever the state of the financial world, it is important to make the best use of financial assets. That is what this book aims to help people to do.

****

Chapter 1

Check Your Bank

How safe is your money? A few years ago, that would have seemed a silly question. Not so silly now, when the government has taken control of two of the leading High Street banks, when banks in the US and Europe, and above all, Iceland, have been going bust.

In the UK, you will get compensation of £85,000 if the bank or building society goes bust - i.e. it cannot return some, or maybe all, of savers' money. Compensation will come from the Financial Services Compensation Scheme (FSCS) and is paid per person per institution. So if you and your partner have a joint account your cover stands at £170,000.

INTEREST INCLUDED

Interest is included in the compensation, so that you do not lose out. If you held a notice account, FSCS reckons that notice was served on the day your account was frozen - and at the end of the notice period you get your capital plus interest. If you had a fixed term account, you get your money, plus interest, on the date it matures.

The basic rule is that the FSCS will cover companies which are regulated by the Financial Services Authority. So, if you join a Xmas hamper scheme, the FSA will not be involved. If that scheme goes broke, you will not get any compensation from the FSCS.

20 DAY LIMIT

But if you have several accounts with the same bank, or group of banks, the compensation applies to all the accounts combined. (Cover applies to private individuals and small companies) Terms of cover were improved last year, when the limit was increased from £50,000. Under the new rules, the FSCS will now pay out within 20 days after the bank goes bust and loans will not be deducted from the compensation - you still owe the money, but it is treated separately.

You may have accounts with banks which are owned by other banks. In that case, you get only one lot of compensation, so you need to be savvy as to who owns whom. If you bank with the Halifax building society, for example, you will be told that Halifax forms part of the Bank of Scotland - so linked to Intelligent Finance and Birmingham Midshires, parts of Lloyds, St James Place, AA savings, SAGA and the Charities Aid Foundation.

BANKS WHICH LOOK ABROAD

What if you put your money with a foreign bank? Though the Iceland banks are long gone, a number of banks operating in the UK look abroad for home. AkBank, Triodos and ING are all Dutch, FirstSave comes from Nigeria, ICICI from India and Citibank from the USA. If a foreign-based bank fails, your best hope is that it is regulated by the Financial Services Authority and is a member of the FSCS.

In that case, you have the same protection as a UK bank account, i.e. the first £85,000 (if you have more than that on deposit you may still get more money back, but you will have to wait your turn in the liquidation process)

THE LOCALS WILL HELP

If you put your money with a European bank which goes bust, you will be covered by the local compensation scheme. Should that pay you less than £85,000, the FSCS will make up the difference (In Iceland's case, the local compensation scheme refused to pay out, so all the liabilities fell on the FSCS and then on the British government). If the bank is not regulated by the FSA and is not a member of the FSCS, then you depend on the local compensation scheme. Remember that the FSCS does not cover deposits outside Europe nor in the Channel Islands or the Isle of Man.(Good news - if you hold foreign currency deposits with a UK bank which fails, you will be repaid in the relevant currency)

One further bit of good news is that this £85,000 compensation also applies to a cash ISA - which, after all, you could regard as a bank account with tax breaks. If an equity ISA fund went bust, the rules are that you would get £50,000. That same £50,000 would apply to a funds platform(think Cofunds or Fidelity)if it went bust while it was still holding investors' money to put into the market. If the funds platform had already bought the shares or units before it went bust, these would just be handed back to you.

When you read investment brochures, check whether FSCS applies. One major bank put out a series of growth plans between 2008 and 2010, stating that customers might be covered if the bank went broke. Earlier this year, it wrote to customers saying that its products would not be covered.

CHECK REGULAR PAYMENTS

So you feel that your bank is safe - or at least you will get enough compensation if they collapse. But what matters for most of us is how we run our day-to-day banking business. To start with, check how much goes out of your account by regular payments:

Standing Order: you tell your bank to pay a fixed amount at regular intervals to a specified person or company - this may be how you give your partner the monthly housekeeping. The bank should not charge you for a standing order. Only you can change it and you can cancel it whenever you like.

Direct Debit: you agree that companies can take fixed or variable amounts from your account - this is the best way to pay credit card bills. You sign a direct debit mandate, and you can cancel at any time. If there is a mistake, the bank picks up the tab.

CONTROL THE DATES

The first step is to ask your bank for a list of these S/Os and DDs, or download if you are into digital banking. Look at the dates - where you can control the payment date, arrange for the debit a few days after your salary arrives. That way, you avoid the risk of inadvertently slipping into the red.

Most important, you need to be clear when regular payments can reduce your bills and where they cost you more. Gas and electricity bills are the most important area where you can make savings by arranging a fixed monthly direct debit - generally around 10% off your bill.

PAY A LUMP SUM

Car insurance works the other way. Many companies will charge you interest if you want to spread your payments rather than pay in a lump sum. Home insurance and your TV licence will also charge.

Always make sure that there is enough in your account to meet the standing orders and direct debits. If your direct debit is returned - i.e. it bounces - you will be hit with a bank charge and your credit rating may start to suffer.

In most financial transactions you can get some protection if you invest through an adviser - compared with a cheaper execution-only intermediary who just does what you tell him. In pensions and insurance, which are difficult technical areas, you will probably need to take advice in any case. You will have someone to look to if the adviser fails to assess how much risk you can take - or if he fails to follow the agreed guidelines - you should be able to go to the Financial Ombudsman.

MONITOR THE RISKS

Most people have now taken on board - especially since the post-2007 crash - that it makes sense to monitor risk. You need to know just how safe is your bank and the risk status of your bond funds and equity unit trusts. There are specialist agencies which monitor risk, such as Moody's, Standard & Poor and Fitch. They also rate countries, which has an immediate impact - a lower credit rating means that the country has to pay a higher rate of interest on its debt. Ireland and Greece were down-rated before their bail-outs; earlier this year Spain and Portugal had their ratings cut back. Any unit trust group should readily give you its credit rating - or you can access it through a financial search engine on the net.

INFLATION: THE REAL THREAT

Losing your savings because a bank or building society goes broke, or being unable to access them for some time, is many people's worst nightmare.

All the post-crunch defences which have been built into the system make this type of disaster much less likely. But danger still lurks - inflation.

We are all caught in a trap. We have to keep some cash, but we are paid tiny amounts by the banks so long as the Bank of England keeps base rate down. When this was written, the best rates on instant access accounts was just under 3%.

USE A CASH ISA

In the meantime, a standard rate taxpayer with the best available instant access account will be getting 2.4% net.(lower figures if you pay 40% or 50%)With inflation at 5.5%, your real capital is slowly and steadily disappearing. You will not pay tax if you hold part of your cash in a cash ISA, where many people keep their short-term funds. But you will still lose out to inflation.

Many people's first reaction is to cut back their cash holdings - not a good idea. The experts suggest that you should keep three to six months' income in cash, available immediately and without penalty. A sudden crisis can happen and there may be opportunities only for people who can put down hard currency. You have to face the certainty that your return will fall behind tax and inflation, but you aim to keep the loss as small as possible. To do that you have to shop around - use newspapers or one of the financial search engines on the net.

MAKE A DIARY NOTE

Two features emerge: the highest rates will be online, as opposed to post and telephone. Then you will find that the most attractive rate includes a 12 month bonus. You may also find that after the 12 months the interest rate drops sharply, so the moral is clear. You put a note in your diary, and just before the 12 months are up you contact the bank - open a new account or take your money elsewhere.

You want instant access for your cash, but you will soon find that you will get a better rate if you are prepared to lock up your money for longer periods - up to five years. The longer the period, the better the rate, but lock up means what it says: you may not be able to access your money at all, or only under penalty, such as giving up six months' interest.

The dilemma is all too simple: you can buy a five-year deposit now and lock in an attractive interest rate. But if interest rates in general start to rise, the rates which look appealing today may be far too low in the world five years from now.

BOND FUNDS SUCCESS

Some banks and building societies offer bonds where the interest is inflation-proofed (see the chapter on The Protected Investor) Many investors, looking for higher yields, have put money into bond funds - one of the great success stories of the last few years. These unit trusts hold company bonds of varying quality, often with a small holding of ordinary shares.

There is a particular benefit when bonds funds are held in an ISA: the manager can reclaim the tax, usually 20% which the paying company deducted (a bond fund, to get this benefit, must be one where at least 60% of the assets are held in bonds). This is a better deal than ordinary shares, where the 10% dividend tax cannot be reclaimed.

YIELD v GROWTH

Bond funds provide attractive yields, generally between 5% and 7%, but they offer limited prospects for capital growth - which is why some bond funds also own ordinary shares. There is risk: yields vary on bond funds, because a bond from a big international group(reckoned to be safe) will yield less than a small overseas company.(regarded as riskier) How to choose? A good place to start is the fund's credit rating, supplied by one of the specialist agencies such as Standard & Poor. You then look at the underlying fund portfolio, most easily accessed over the net.

You will find that bonds are ranked three ways: investment grade, high yield and junk.

THE THREE TYPES

Investment grade means bonds issued by the government (gilt-edged in the UK)and major companies. High yield bonds are issued by smaller companies or foreign entities. Junk means what it says - in particular, financial markets think there is a risk that the company or country will default.

As so often, you get what you pay for. There is a clear trade-off between yield and risk - low yield= low risk, high yield= high risk. Which you choose depends on your needs and judgment. If you find it difficult to choose - you need the income, but worry about the risk - why not buy a mixture?

LISTING IS THE DIFFERENCE

There is one fundamental difference between a bond fund and a bank deposit, of whatever length. Your bond fund is listed on the stock market, so the value of your investment will fluctuate. With a bank deposit, the value of your capital is assured - at least its nominal, if not its real, value. Bond fund prices will fall when interest rates rise and they will go up when rates fall. High yield bonds, issued by medium-sized rather than large companies, will do better when the economy is in a growth phase. Investment grade bonds, issued by the strongest companies, should hold up during a recession.

****

Chapter 2

The Protected Investor

If only, you say, there was a way to protect your savings income from inflation. If only, you add, there was a way to invest in shares so that you could protect your capital from loss. Now, you can meet both of these objectives. There are costs - you have to decide, given your own situation and personal preference, whether the protection is worth it.

Index-linked gilt-edged are available, but this has always been a professionals' market.

Pending the return of index-linked certificates - and the chance to examine the new small print - financial companies such as building societies have stepped into the market. You can choose a bond or a deposit where interest is inflation-linked - though your capital remains unchanged and open to price inflation.

INFLATION-FREE INTEREST

An interest-proofed bond will run for five years, with no access allowed or only under penalty. The minimum subscription will range between £500 and £3,000 and you will be able to put the bond into a cash ISA - so that interest will come to you free of tax and free of inflation. For 2011-12 you can put £5,340(half of your total allowance) into a cash ISA, and your partner can do the same.

The bond will give you a low basic rate of interest, say 1.5% over the five years. At the end of the five years, your return equals the increase in inflation plus the small basic rate. A plus feature is that these bonds reckon by the Retail Prices Index - rather than the Consumer Price Index, used by the Bank of England, which gives lower figures.

CAPITAL STAYS THE SAME

This means that if inflation hits 20% over the five years, you will receive that amount in interest plus the 1.5%, making a total £2,150 on an investment of £10,000. You get your capital back, but only the amount you invested - that has not been inflation-proofed. If inflation is nil or negative, as it was during the crunch, then you get the 1.5%, equal to £150 on a £10,000 investment. Even at today's low rates, you would have done better to put your money into an ordinary cash deposit account over the same period.

As a variant to the bond, you could take out a five-year account, divided into five annual periods. At the end of each annual period your interest will amount to the rise in the Retail Prices Index plus a basic 0.1%. This means that, if inflation hits 5% over the year (the annual rate when this was written) your income will total £510 on a £10,000 investment. If inflation is nil or negative over the year, you get the basic 0.1% - so just 10.

SHARES WITH PROTECTION

But you may worry about protecting your capital if inflation remains around current levels. The traditional wisdom is that you should buy shares - or unit trusts which hold shares - as the best available protection. If you buy shares, and you are unlucky or make mistakes, you could lose some of your initial investment. You ask: how to square the circle - buy shares and protect your capital?

Answer: you invest in a protected, or guaranteed, investment plan. This is what a typical plan looks like:

o You put up a minimum investment, usually between £2,000 and £5,000.

o The plan will typically run for five years - sometimes as short as three years or as long as six or seven.

o You will be paid the percentage growth in the FTSE index of the London stock market, up to a maximum f 50%.

o At the end of the five years, even if the stock market has fallen 50% - in fact, however much it falls - you get your capital back.

o You may be able to put your plan into an ISA, so that all the gains would come free of tax.

So you seem to have squared the circle - though you need to remember that no two guaranteed plans are necessarily the same, using different indexes and different payout rates. Under this typical plan, the major appeal is that there is no chance of losing your original investment, even if the stock market goes into free-fall. If the stock market booms, you will take home £150 for every £100 which you invested. This looks good, but you know that every investment has its pros and cons. For protected plans, there are typically four cons:

• Lack of flexibility. Your money is locked up for five years, or whatever is the life of the plan. You may have no access to your capital at all - or only by paying a penalty, maybe losing some capital protection.

- No dividends. You will not receive any dividends or interest over the five years. If the shares represented in your plan yield 4%, you are giving up that amount, compounded, over the five years - a significant sum.

- Tax. All gains from the plan are taxed as income, not CGT. Putting your plan investment into an ISA, which is possible with most schemes, would solve this problem. But if you invest outside an ISA, you need to recognise that, if the plan works in your favour, you stand to receive a lump of taxable income at the end of the five years. If you are a 20% taxpayer this could push you into the 40% band and perhaps even from 40% to the top 50%.

- Inflation. If the stock market crashes, you get all of your capital back - but this is the money capital which you invested five years before. What you get back will be reduced in real terms by five years of inflation - running around 5% a year when this was written. Look for schemes which add some interest to your investment if they have to hand your capital back to you, with no gain, when the index crashes.

'KICK-OUT' CAN HELP

People also comment on the charges which investors suffer on protected plans, that the costs are sometimes not wholly transparent, and that the brochures inevitably contain a generous quota of small print. One important item in the small print is how the index is calculated in order to decide how much you get when the plan matures. This is generally worked out in the last year from an average of the last 12 monthly readings, but some plans include a .kick-out' provision which gives you the maximum pay-out if the index hits the key number before the plan matures.

'Kick-out' is a useful feature to look for, as it aims to solve one obvious problem - that the stock market may boom during the first few years of your five-year plan, but drop like a stone in the last 12 months, leaving you with a small gain and regrets for missed opportunities. "Kick-out' works like this: suppose that you have a five-year plan where the maximum growth in the index is set at 50%. The fund (or that section of it) will be closed, and you will be repaid, if the index registers a 50% gain at pre-determined points in the intervening years. Absent a 'kick-out,' you would just have to watch the stock market take off before it fell back, while your neighbour was cashing in the tracker units which he bought as an alternative.

BETTER THAN 100%

Gearing-up is another feature to look for is when schemes offer you better than 100% of the rise in the stock market index. You may be capped at a 50% gain, but some schemes will offer you say 1.5 times the index growth: when the stock market moves upwards, that means you will hit your maximum much more quickly.

That has appeal, especially when linked to a 'kick-out' arrangement. Most protection schemes cover the share index of the London stock market, but there are also plans which are based on say three international indexes. You could also put money into a scheme which is based on house prices - using one of the principal house price indexes, which come from Halifax and Nationwide. Using these schemes of this sort can help give you a diversified, so better balanced, portfolio.

Some investors look at protected share plans as savings accounts where the return is based on the stock market rather than Bank of England base rate. If you take out a five-year plan, capped at a 50%

rise in the index, and it hits the maximum, then you will make 8.45% a year compounded. You would still get 3.71% if the index managed only a 20% gain.

WHO PROTECTS?

One fundamental question is - who gives the guarantee or protection? Usually, this will come from one of the leading UK banks - if they go bust, you will get compensation from the Financial Services Compensation Scheme, so at worst you may have to wait a little time for your money (this has been speeded up since the banks got into crunch-time difficulties) A few years ago, some investors were startled to find that their protected schemes were covered by Lehman, the US/UK bank which fell into spectacular bankruptcy.

Rather less appealing is when the guarantee comes from a subsidiary of a UK bank which is based offshore. Investors cam remember that when the Iceland banks hit problems, compensation worked rather better onshore UK than in some overseas banking centres.

READ THE SMALL PRINT

Under these schemes, you know that you cannot lose - whatever happens to the stock market, you are certain that you will get your money back. But this certainty comes at a cost and you may wonder if you are paying too much, so you look at the options. The first option is to read all the small print and distinguish between:

(1)protected schemes where you could lose some, maybe all, of your money if the stock market goes into a serious nose-dive, and
(2)guaranteed schemes where you get your money back whatever happens to the stock market.

Guaranteed share schemes do a better job at preserving your investment, but the terms may mean that they will cost you more. As ever, you are looking at a trade-off and you have to reach your own decision.

OR A GUARANTEE FROM YOUR COMPANY

If you work for a business which has a stock exchange listing, you will probably be able to set up your own loss-proof plan - Save As You Earn. Shares are allotted to you below the stock market price, and you can invest between £5 and £250 a month. You can choose a scheme which runs for three, five or seven years.

The joy of SAYE is that when the plan matures, you have a choice. You can take cash, or you can invest in the shares. You cannot lose - though later on, if you want to sell the shares, remember that you will be inline for CGT. But you do not have to sell all the shares at once, you can move them into joint ownership with your partner - and you have the CGT-free annual exemption.

There is also a useful Share Incentive Plan which can give you up to £3,000 of free shares a year, plus another two shares for each one you buy - up to a maximum £6,000 of free shares. This plan has to be open to all employees on similar terms, with the big attraction that it comes tax and NI free if you hold for five years.

CHECK THE OPTIONS

Whether you want to inflation-proof your savings interest, or buy shares only when your capital can be protected, has to a question of your own investment style and your own circumstances. But it makes sense, if only as a way to check the options, to match these schemes against run-of-the-mill investment decisions.

Your neighbour, who avoids investment schemes but shares your worries, might do two things. First, he could invest in high-yielding equities: the high yield should act as some defence against a fall in the stock market, while the equities will give some help against inflation. Second, he could buy into one of several unit trusts which offer a 80-20 or similar bond/equity mix. As an alternative, he might put together an international portfolio, again mixing bonds and shares.

When this was written, it was possible to buy these types of unit trust offering dividend yields ahead of inflation - no guarantees or protection or inflation-proofing, but also no extra costs.

****

Chapter 3

Get Plastic to Help

Credit cards offer a way to make significant financial gains, if you are prepared to take just a little trouble. All you need to do is work to a diary - and keep up an average interest in saving money. You do not need to be a credit card nerd.

It will be more difficult to benefit from credit cards if you owe money on cards or if you have a patchy credit history. If you owe money on cards, you will probably be paying a double-digit rate of interest, so it makes sense to clear what you owe, through a bank loan or overdraft or using other cards. If your credit history is not as good as you would like, the best way forward is to rebuild your story - take out a new card and spend a year behaving like the perfect card user.

RATES ARE HIGH

This tells you, at the start, two things you should avoid doing with your card. You should not borrow, except for very short periods, simply because the interest rates are high. Rates can be even higher on store cards than on regular credit cards. Remember: the card company will charge you if you pay late, if you go beyond your credit limit, if any payment is returned unpaid (including a balance transfer)or if the card company serves a default notice.

You should not use your card to draw cash, just because interest rates are high and your account may be debited when you draw the cash - rather than the later date of your account. To draw cash in the UK or abroad, use a debit card.

There are four ways you can gain a money benefit from your credit card. For the first, start with the statement you receive every month. You will have checked to make sure that all the charges are in order(more on this later)but your first step is to note the date when payment is due. You then focus on the date of the statement.

INTEREST-FREE DAYS

The interest-free period on the card, which can be up to 50-55 days, runs from the statement date. This means that if you use the card immediately after the statement date, you will have gained extra weeks of free credit. And free credit means money in the bank.

So you postpone a major purchase until just after, rather than just before, the statement date. But the real scope comes when, like most of us, you have two or three cards. These will have different statement dates (some cards let you fix your own date when you join)so you work them together. Do it simply: when a statement arrives, use that card until the next statement from another card, when you switch to them. In this way, you keep the interest-free period rolling forward.

CASH BACK CARDS

The second way to benefit from cards applies to people who pay off all their credit card bills each month. If you are one of these, then you should arrange to get money back (If you repay only part of your bill, the interest cost will wipe out the cash back benefit). One leading card offers you a 1% cash back on everything you buy(though not money transfers)which you get as a deduction once a year from your monthly bill.

American Express, at the time of writing, offered the best cash back terms, at 5% for three months and then a tiered refund. Use the net to check out the best offer.

As an alternative to cash, some cards will give you air miles or points which you can spend in high street stores. All the major store cards (Tesco, John Lewis, Marks & Spencer) give you points when you use their card in store. You will get a lower rate when you use the card somewhere else, though some cards, such as Boots, can only be used in store.

VOUCHER TO HELP

Every few months the store adds up the points on your card and sends you a voucher which will help pay for the next bill. If you are a regular shopper at the store, these deals are a benefit: you get what amount to a discount when you would have shopped there any way. You just need to check store cards against cashback: you should be getting between 0.5% and 1% - if not, then switch from your store card to cash back. Some store cards will be sold to you on the spot when you shop, offering say a 10-15% discount on what you are buying - the sales assistant will arrange the deal while you wait. It makes sense to take the price incentive, plus maybe other benefits such as special shopping days, but do not borrow: store cards charge high interest rates.

0% INTEREST SHOPPING

Using a cash back card or a store card is good, but you can go a step further: you can shop for up to a year at 0% interest. Several cards offer new customers 0% deals, typically for nine to 12 months: you can buy what you want up to your credit limit, you will not be charged interest and all you have to pay back over the period is the monthly minimum. You will not be able to use a card which you already hold - or have recently held - and your credit score should be good enough to support a new card application.

Under a 0% shopping deal, you are being offered a sizeable interest-free loan, which has to be good news. You could, in theory, set aside every month the amount which you would normally have paid: the interest you receive will measure the benefit you gained from the card company. In a 0% shopping deal, it is important to keep within the rules - not to exceed your credit limit and not to miss the monthly payment (so set up a direct debit). If you do break one of the rules, it will probably cost you, it will not help your credit score and the card company may be entitled to cancel the whole deal.

WHEN THE DEAL ENDS

After 12 months, when the 0% deal comes to an end, you owe the card company for all the goodies you bought less the 25% or so which you paid off through the monthly minimum payments. If you do nothing, the card company will switch you to its normal lending rate, which means that you will find yourself paying 15% or more, compared with zero!

You know that if you pay 15% a debt will double every five years - something you wish to avoid. Maybe you set aside enough cash over the year, or maybe you spent it. To repay what you owe, you could move your debt to another card company, who will also charge you 0%. You will pay a fee, but you will have a further year to ponder your new interest-free loan. You are looking at balance transfer.

0% BALANCE TRANSFERS

A balance transfer means precisely what it says. You transfer the balance from your old card to the new one, who have agreed to charge you 0% for 12 months. In return, they will charge you a fee of 2-3%. You can continue to make balance transfers once your current one runs out - provided that your credit history will support the new cards which you will need, and so long as attractive deals are available.

When you took out a balance transfer, the advice used to be - get another card for your normal buying, because when you pay off debt the card company will first pay off the low-interest debt, leaving you with the high-interest. Just recently, however, the card companies have agreed with the government to pay off the debt in sequence, starting with the most expensive. Good news; you need to check.

COMPANIES MORE SELECTIVE

Some people miss out on 0% shopping or balance transfers because their card application is turned down - and in tougher economic times, the card companies have become more selective. If you do fail the credit score, the card company does not have to explain why though you may find a clue by testing your score on the net.

There may be a simple mistake, which you can find on your credit file -in any case, it makes sense to access your file, which is easy and costs very little. Go to one of the three major credit agencies, who will send you a copy of your file for a few pounds. They may be prepared to e-mail you whenever the file changes. If there is a mistake on your file, you have the legal right to have this corrected.

COVER WHEN THERE'S CREDIT

Credit cards can also help protect you from the fall-out of fraud or a tough economic climate. As most people know by now, you should use a credit card when making a large purchase - not just goods, but also say an air ticket or a package holiday.

Under the Consumer Credit Act 1974, the credit card company is jointly responsible with the seller, in any deal between £100 and £30,000, for any misrepresentation or breach of contract. This applies both in the UK and overseas. In a typical case, you pay a deposit on some furniture which does not arrive because the store has since gone broke. You become an unsecured creditor, which almost certainly means that you have lost your money. But as you used a credit card, the card company will pay you back.

OR CHARGEBACK

Strictly speaking, this protection only applies where this a credit element. So if you used a charge card or a debit card or a credit card cheque, rather than a credit card you will not be covered by the legislation. But there is still hope: the banks have developed a chargeback system, which is intended to cover these non credit deals and credit card deals which fall below the £100 lower limit.

If you want to claim under chargeback, you should first contact the bank which provides your card. They go to the seller's bank, and you should get the refund from them. You may have to persevere, as chargeback is relatively new. In the last resort, you can take your case to the Financial Ombudsman - as you can with any credit card dispute.

USING YOUR CARD ABROAD

We all use our credit cards when we go abroad on holiday - when we may be paying an unnecessary charge. (First step is to tell the card company where and when you are going: they might just decide to block your card when they see unusual spending). The great majority of credit card companies make a charge, usually between 2.5% and 3%, when they convert your foreign spending into sterling to make up your monthly bill. The same charge arises when you use your credit card over the net to buy something which is priced in dollars or euros. On a £800 holiday spend you will pay an extra £20-£25.

SOME WAIVE FEES

Several cards do not charge on currency deals - some waive the fee just in Europe, others round the world. You need to check against your travel plans. When this was written, credit cards which waived all or some of the currency charge included Halifax, Nationwide, Post Office and Saga(for the over 50s). You will not use your credit card to draw cash abroad - except in an emergency - but using a debit card will still leave you open to the currency surcharge. One solution is to open a bank account with one of the companies which does not make a currency charge and use their debit card abroad. That works, but is cumbersome. How to take money abroad is discussed in the next chapter, which looks at loaded or prepaid cards. But loaded cards can be useful even if you are not going abroad.

OR A LOADED CARD?

The theory of the loaded card is simple: you put in cash, so you are free to spend and to draw cash from an ATM. There is no credit.

35

But just because your credit status is not involved, there is no bank check when you apply for the card, which makes the process simpler. As you can only spend what you put in, you are operating to a budget which some people find helpful - though it is easy to re-load the card by phone or over the net.

Loaded cards also come in useful when you finance a student son or daughter or when they go backpacking. If a villain steals your loaded card, or they get hold of the key data, you cannot lose more than the amount which remains on the card. The villain cannot clean out your bank account, which he might be able to do by stealing your debit card. You will face some costs, and you need to check how much and when - when you set up the card, when you close it, when you draw from an ATM. You are not likely to get any interest on the money which you load into the card.

THINK CARD SECURITY

Loaded cards can make security easier to deal with - which is useful, because credit card security is a growing problem. There are a few basic rules: look after your cards and if you lose one, phone the card company immediately. There are card security businesses which will help for a small fee.(Security issues in general are covered in a later chapter).

Always read your monthly card statement; if you see something you do not recognise, phone the card company. It may be harmless - the company which gets the money is not the one which sold you the goods but if in doubt, phone, and note your phone call. (Fraudsters sometimes slip in small amounts which they hope you will not notice) When you no longer need the card statements, put them in a shredder or chop them up with a pair of scissors.

Above all, make sure your PIN is secure and keep the number strictly to yourself. If the card company or the insurer thinks that you have passed on your PIN, even unintentionally, you could face problems when you seek compensation for losses. You want to protect yourself and you have to treat the card company with reasonable care. Just be careful: it's your money.

****

Chapter 4

Look After Your Savings

You have saved over the years, postponing or giving up things you would have liked to do and stuff you would have liked to buy. You want your savings, at the least, to keep up with inflation - you want them to grow over the years. So how do you do it?

You start with your cash buffer, which is equal to between three and six month's income and probably sits in cash ISAs. These are tax-free, but their yield is well below the current rate of inflation - and, like every cash fund, they offer no prospect of capital growth. You need this cash cushion to deal with emergencies and to take advantage of any opportunities that come along. The ISAs will look better, performance-wise, if shares and house prices start to fall.

As a first step, you need to work out where you are going:

OBJECTIVE: you have to be clear what you are saving for. It may be to pay for the kids through university, it may be to go on a cruise round the world or it may be simply to buy a better pension and have a happier retirement. Only you can decide what it is you want, but you need to set your objective, because that will determine the other two issues - timing and risk.

TIMING: your time horizon will follow from your objective, and will determine which investments you buy. If your time horizon is short - say five years before the kids go to university - most of your money will go into bonds and fixed interest. If you are in your 40s, planning to retire in 20 years' time, most of your money will go into shares or property: years of inflation will cripple the value of cash and bonds.

RISK: this has to be the amount of risk and uncertainty which you can live with. Some people accept high risk, with the prospect of high reward - which may or may not happen. If you are happy to take risks, you buy shares because there is a rumour of a take-over, you prefer a small oil producer in central Asia to investing in Shell or BP. The only test is performance, i.e. what works. How you get there has to be, to some degree, a matter of taste.

ASSETS TO CHOOSE

For the average investor, there is a choice of four assets which will grow your savings - shares/unit trusts, bonds, property and cash. Wealthy private investors and investment institutions, such as pension funds and insurance companies, have a wider choice. They can go out and buy a commodity like oil or take over a factory estate: as they are big, they deal in large amounts and they are better able to cope with risk.

SHARES/UNIT TRUSTS: what the stock market calls equities, which you can buy direct or though a pooled vehicle, i.e. a unit trust. Shares are the traditional long-term investment as they take part in the growth of business and the economy. Studies by Barclays bank show that share prices in London have risen an average 5% a year over the last 110 years. On Wall Street, shares have risen an average 7% a year since that market opened in 1792.

Shares and share-backed unit trusts are still the outstanding long-term investment: shares and property are the only ones of the four asset types(shares/unit trusts, bonds, property, cash)which offer the prospect of capital growth. But - and this is a big but - shares' recent track record is not so good. An investor who bought shares at the end of 1999 would still be showing a small loss, no less than 12 years on! As all the ads tell you, share prices can go down as well as up - but for the average investor, shares have to be the principal way to benefit from the growth of businesses and the economy.

BONDS: these are fixed-interest IOUs issued by governments and companies.(UK government bonds are called gilt-edged or gilts)Bonds are safer than shares - they have a prior claim on the company's assets - and typically have a fixed life, of around 20 years. During these years a bond will give you a fixed income, generally much more than a share, but there is little prospect of any capital gain. Bond prices will rise when interest rates fall, and vice versa. Bonds will give you a high, relatively safe income - which is why so many people rushed into bond funds when the yields on cash fell low.

PROPERTY: most of us are property investors through our own home, and some people carry the idea a stage further through buy-to-let. This involves buying houses and flats, often with a large mortgage, to let to tenants such as nurses and students. For investors, property usually means commercial property - shops, offices and factories which are often let to government departments or big companies. Commercial property comes in large amounts, so the only access for an average investors is though a unit or investment trust.

One point to watch is that the trust keeps sufficient cash, otherwise there may be a logjam if a number of people want to sell their units at the same time.

CASH: as a prudent investor, you have your buffer which is equal to three or six months' income. As the yields on cash are so low, you will hold large amounts of cash only when you think your other assets are going to lose their value.(We all know that putting cash under the mattress is a bad financial idea: there is no yield, so its real value drops and there is always the risk that someone will find your stash) Really clever people will then use the cash to buy back at a lower price the investments they had previously sold - which is how hedge funds made so much money from bank shares.

INVEST BY AGE

There are a few basic rules about investment. One of the oldest is that your age, in years, equals the percentage of your investments that you should put into fixed interest bonds. At age 40, with 20 years to go to retirement, your assets would be split 40-60 between bonds and shares. By age 60, under this rule, the numbers are reversed: you are 60% in bonds and 40% in shares.

This makes sense: by age 60 your shares have less time to grow in value, and as you are about to retire, maybe buy an annuity, you need the more secure value of bonds. This is the .lifestyle' change which is followed by insurance companies and fund managers. You start by being mainly invested in equities and gradually move into bonds as the years go by.

Everyone, except for the seriously well-off, will invest in bonds and property through a unit trust: the size of the investment is just so large. You can invest in shares the same way: you choose the unit trust which fits with your strategic thinking (how you should buy into a unit trust - see later in this chapter) and you then access a spread of investments and full-time professional help.

OR GO FOR SHARES

Some people like to buy individual shares - they know the company or it is recommended by someone whose views they trust. If you go for shares, you will need to buy a number just to give you a spread of risk: never forget that, in investment you should not put all your eggs in one basket.

If you buy shares, you will need to go to a stockbroker. If you know what you want to do, you will choose an execution-only broker. You will not get any advice (though he may pass on financial data)and you will find this represents the lowest-cost route. (Dealing online costs less than over the telephone) If you want the broker to advise you, you have a choice.

WITH ADVICE?

You can opt for advice, where he contacts you with ideas and does not act unless you agree. Alternatively, you can arrange a discretionary relationship: you sort out guidelines and agree cash limits with the broker, who is then free to act without checking with you beforehand. In any case, you will get a contract note which will give details of the deal.

You may feel baffled by financial planning and reckon that you need wide-ranging advice. In that case, you will look for an independent financial adviser (IFA). An IFA will cost, either by charging you a fee or (at present) taking a commission on the assets which he persuades you to buy. A good financial adviser will save you time and money. Unless you know one, or one is strongly recommended, this is what you should do.

o Think carefully what type of advice you need and what exactly you expect to get.

o Contact at least three firms and compare their costs (reckon up to £200 an hour) and the services they offer.

o Get the adviser's recommendations in writing - if there is anything you do not understand, get the adviser to explain.

o Spend time on the .fact find' which the adviser must prepare - this shows your income and expenditure, your commitments and your objectives, all of which form the basis of his advice to you.

BUY INTO MANAGEMENT SKILLS

People who buy into unit trusts do so partly because of the underlying fund management skills. This is the "active management" for which the investor will typically pay a 5% entry fee plus a annual management fee of 1.5%. These charges can impact performance - the Financial Services Authority suggests that you assume 6% yearly growth in shares, which is just a little more than Barclays' 110 year average. On these numbers, you would give up the first year's performance and a quarter for each of the remaining years.

Or you can opt for "passive management" - a tracker unit trust, which tracks a particular index. There is no management required: the manager devises a computer program or buys the shares which make up the particular index. You can track the FTSE 100, 250 or 350 or the market as a whole, or the US or Europe.

TRACKERS COST LESS

As a result, a tracker unit trust is low cost (but check: not all of them charge low fees). During the first year in an actively managed fund you would pay 6.5%. In a tracker you would generally face no initial charge and an annual cost of no more than 0.5%. So in that case the traditional unit trust is charging you 13 times more in fees than a tracker.

But the active manager, you reply, will more than make up this cost by out-performing the index. But will he? There are outstanding fund managers, such as Neil Woodford and Anthony Bolton - who returned an average of 19.5% a year over a 28 year period running the Fidelity special situations fund. But the average picture is different. Advisers regularly publish lists of .dog' funds and the Sandler report to the Treasury showed that over a 10 year period the average UK unit trust underperformed the market by as much as 2.5% a year. So you could pay a lot less for a tracker unit trust which performed a lot better.

You have two issues in choosing the right active manager. One is to find the right person - preferably before everyone else does. Secondly, you have to be sure that he will continue to be the right person through the stock market's ups and downs. (Advisers report when people change jobs). History may not help: when the FSA looked into this area, they found that fund managers with strong track records are no more likely to achieve better returns in the future than poor historical performers.

PERHAPS AN ETF?

A unit trust tracker has appeal, but many people would prefer a fund that could also track oil or gold and where the units could be traded instantly, like shares. This is the ETF, the Exchange Traded Fund.

ETFs have boomed over recent years - one of the largest UK funds is now an ETF which tracks the US stock market. ETFs, like unit trust trackers, are low cost but can be complex - especially those that invest direct in commodities, and those which are leveraged, i.e. they deliver a multiple of the performance of the underlying index. Buying an ETF which invests in oil may appeal, but remember that the ETF will not own the oil: the fund will track contracts which are based on the underlying commodity.

CHARGES - HOW TO REDUCE THEM

After all this, you may decide that a particular actively managed fund is the one for you. But you do not like the charging set-up, where the fees may cost you most, maybe all, of the first year's performance and a £10,000 investment would be hit by £650 of first year costs.

There are two ways to cut the cost of unit trust buying. One is to go to a fund supermarket, where you will pay a smaller initial charge and be able to mix and match a range of investments. The supermarket may also simplify your life by handling paperwork and collecting dividends.

The second way to cut costs is to go to a discount broker - who may also run his own supermarket. The discount broker will cut all, or most, of the initial fee and he may pass on some of his .trail commission.' This arises because the fund manager gives the broker a small annual commission, normally 0.5%, so long as you keep the units which you bought. Some brokers will share this trail commission with you, in the form of a loyalty bonus, and you may even be able to get it all - not a fortune, but safe and steady earner.

TAX NOT THE DRIVER

Another old, but sensible investment proverb is that you should not make investments primarily for tax reasons. That makes sense, but you need to appreciate that tax will make a difference, unless you invest through a tax-free SIPP or an ISA. Investment professionals talk about the .total return' on shares, meaning capital and dividend growth together - but remember that on capital growth you pay tax up to 28%, while on income you could pay nearly double that, up to 50%.

All share dividends come with a 10% tax credit. But that credit cannot be claimed back, even if you hold the shares in a tax-free ISA. When you get a dividend, the amount of tax you pay depends on your place in the tax scale. There is a concession for small savers with little other income: a special tax rate of 10% up to £2,560 for this tax year - but the 10% rate will not apply if the individual's other non-savings income is above that limit.

This is what you pay on dividends:

Standard Rate -
up to £35,000 a year 10%
Higher Rate -
£35,001 to £150,000 32.5%
Additional Rate -
over £150,000 42.5%

Dividends are treated as the top slice of total income, savings as the next slice and other income as the lowest slice.

CHOOSING TAX-FREE

For an ISA, tax-free is not strictly accurate - you are not free of the 10% dividend charge - but you pay no more tax. For people who pay higher rate tax and above (i.e. anyone who makes more than £35,000 a year) there is strong case for taking out an ISA, an Individual Savings Account, every tax year. An ISA is a wrapper where you can put shares and bonds and then stay free of any further tax.

USE IT OR LOSE IT!

For 2011-12 you can put £10,680 into an ISA and that limit will be increased every year in line with inflation. The limit does not run from one year to the next - use it or lose it! You can put up to half into a cash ISA and the rest into a stocks and shares ISA, which includes bonds. Or you can put the whole amount into a stocks and shares ISA.

Bonds are a good fit for ISAs, as the fund manager can reclaim tax provided his fund holds a minimum 60% bonds.(If you want to change your ISA manager, that can easily be done)You may not set up a joint ISA with your partner, but each of you can have your own. You can open a cash ISA at age 16 and a share/bond ISA from age 18.

NOW A JUNIOR ISA

From November 1, ISA's will become even bigger when Junior ISA's replace Child Trust Funds-family and friends of all under-18's who do not have a CTF will be able to put in up to £3,600 of cash and shares each year, bringing all the benefits of an adult ISA. The money will be locked away until the youngster reaches age 18, though they will be able to manage the account once they reach 16. (A sixteen year old can take out a cash ISA, so here is the chance of two sets of tax-free allowances for two years).

The government reckons that six-million boys and girls will be eligible when junior ISA's are launched, with another 800,000 a year becoming eligible after that. Experts calculate that regular contributions over 18 years, assuming interest growth of 7% a year, would produce a pot of just over £150,000. That should cope with university fees or provide the deposit for a first time house purchase.

PREMIUM BONDS - STILL WORTH IT?

Once upon a time, tax-free investment for many people would have meant buying premium bonds. But lower interest rates have hit premium bonds - because there is now a smaller pot from which to pay the prizes. The Treasury sets a rate of interest; that rate is applied every month to all the bonds, and that in turn determines the size of the prize fund. The lower the rate, the smaller the prize fund.

At present, the rate for the prize fund stands at 1.5% a year. There is a monthly prize of £1 million, and minimum prizes of £25 - National Savings seem to follow a policy of more prizes rather than bigger prizes. You can buy up to £30,000 worth of premium bonds and you do not even have to report prizes to the taxman. The chances of becoming an instant millionaire have great appeal. But at today's interest rates the odds are heavily stacked against you.

SMALL AND FRIENDLY

If the notion of safe tax-free investment appeals to you, think about friendly societies. Because they enjoy tax breaks, the Treasury limits the amount you can save to only £270 a year - though you can include your partner and any under 16s.

Friendly societies will sell you a 10-year insurance policy, maybe linked to a tracker unit trust. Some societies will allow you to make a one-off payment to cover premiums for 10 years. Friendly societies are safe and small - but a mini-step in the right direction.

****

Chapter 5

When Your Holiday Costs More-What Can You Do

Currencies fluctuate. Not so many years ago, your £100 would have given you only about 100 US dollars. Move on a short time, it would have given you 200 dollars. Now, it gives you around 160. The euro, in its short life, has also shifted around. For several years, a bill for 100 euros would have cost you around £70.

Then sterling weakened, so 100 euros cost you almost £100. Since then the euro has weakened, so that 100 euros would now set you back about £85. Some of these changes took time - others just a few days.

Why do currencies fluctuate and what can you do about it? Here are some reasons why values vary:

Economics: when big problems arise, the currency will suffer. The euro was hit because Greece had a budget issue: the pound suffered because two of the big problem banks were British.

Finance: when a country cuts interest rates, the currency will fall because assets there earn less. This helps to explain the pound's weakness - reckoned to be part deliberate in order to make UK exports cheaper.

Politics: when a change of government looks likely, the currency will stall. Foreign exchange markets, like all markets, hate uncertainty. Pro-democracy protests in Egypt and Tunisia hit their currencies.

Psychology: when there are serious worldwide problems, people turn to the one world currency - the US dollar. Many countries hold their reserves in dollars - and you can use dollar bills in many places outside the USA. When the dollar itself has problems, people turn to gold.

TRY POUND AVERAGING

So how do you know when to buy? You don't - nor does anybody else. People tackle this thorny question in two ways. One is to look at history and buy your holiday currency when it looks cheap by recent years' standards. It may get cheaper still, but there is no way to be certain. The second way is to go in for pound averaging: you know roughly how much currency you are going to need, so you buy 25% of that amount every three months in the year before you go. Pound averaging is an established stock market technique which forms the basis for share savings plans: you may not hit the best rate over the year, but you should avoid the worst.

So you go ahead and buy your holiday currency. There is one fundamental rule when you buy: check the rate. In currency deals the exchange rate is what matters. You can check by telephone or most simply over the net. Many companies will offer you currency free of commission - but you may get a worse rate than a rival who charges commission. As always, you need to be sure that there are no hidden charges. To get the best deal, here are some do's and don'ts:

DO check if the company will buy currency back from you - free of commission, if you bought that way -when you come back from your holiday. Some will guarantee to buy back at a rate which is at least as good as when you bought. If you come back with a small amount of currency, keep it for your next trip: remember that changing currency will cost through the .spread' - the difference between the supplier's buying and selling price.

DON'T leave currency buying until the last minute, when you get to the airport - this is probably the most expensive route. Whether you buy what you need in one deal, or spread the buying over a period, you should have all that you need in place a few days before you leave.

DO check the currency rates you get on the net with those you are offered on the High Street. The net offers competitive exchange rates, and some of the suppliers will deliver for free if you buy £500 worth of currency.

On the high street, it may be worth haggling - some suppliers will adjust their rates if you find a better deal elsewhere.

DON'T pay commission on foreign currency unless you are offered a clearly good rate of exchange. Remember that the suppliers who offer commission-free deals make their money on the buy/sell spread.

Which underlines the basic rule: what the deal comes down to is the rate you are being offered. (Remember that the buy/sell spreads will be smallest on major currencies such as the dollar and the euro, where turnover is huge; you will pay more to buy and sell less well-known currencies)

So you have your foreign currency - and you have insurance cover if the cash is lost or stolen, from travel insurance or maybe from your home contents policy. How much cash you take depends on where you go and the type of holiday you take. In faraway places(and faraway from an ATM)you will need more cash. In parts of Asia and South America it is often a good idea to take some small US dollar bills.(An especially good idea when you find that the currency at your destination is not available outside that country).

EXTRA RIGHTS FOR PACKAGE HOLIDAYS

Many people like to book a package holiday, where it is useful to know that you have important extra rights. (A package holiday is pre-arranged, sold for an inclusive price and likely to include transport and accommodation - as opposed to when you book the parts of your holiday separately).

To start with, your package deal must spell out how the price can be changed. So your first step is to check the small print of the contract. The operator himself has to absorb the first 2% of any price increase - and he can only alter the price when there is a change in the cost of transport, fees and taxes or a shift in the exchange rate. And he cannot change the price within 30 days of your departure.

If the package operator meets these tests and wants to raise the price by 10% or more, you will probably be able to choose an alternative holiday or cancel and ask for a refund. If you cancel, you may be able to claim back incidental costs, such as buying holiday currency.

AVOID THE ADD-ON

Assuming that you head for Europe or North America, most of your holiday spending will be paid for by credit card. This area is covered in the chapter on credit cards, but it is so important to be worth repeating. Most credit cards charge an extra 2.5-3% when they convert your holiday spend into sterling. Some cards do not impose this charge: so use one of those. These include SAGA for the over 50s, Halifax, Nationwide and the Post Office.

When you need cash, you will use a debit card - not a credit card - at the local ATMs. And you will avoid the extra 2.5-3% charge by setting up an account before you leave.(If you use a credit card, you could be charged interest from the date of the transaction - even if you pay your card bills in full) As a simpler alternative, you could use a loaded, i.e. prepaid, card: see later in this chapter.

When you are abroad, some hotels and restaurants may ask if you, as their valued British guest, would prefer to have the bill made out in sterling. Say No! This is no favour to you - known in the trade as .dynamic currency conversion.'

If you accepted, you might just find that your host had turned your bill into sterling at an eye-watering rate of exchange!

MAYBE THINK TRAVELLER'S CHEQUES

Many people prefer not to take large amounts of cash abroad, for the obvious security risk. If you are concerned that credit cards may not be widely accepted - outside major towns in many countries - you need to look at the options. Traveller's cheques are the traditional alternative to cash: these are issued say by American Express or Thomas Cook and you can choose from among several leading currencies.

Traveller's cheques are easy to use: you sign them when you buy and when you want cash abroad you just countersign and show some ID. They do not have an expiry date, and security is good. You note the numbers of the cheques and if they are lost or stolen you will get a replacement, maybe within 24 hours in Europe and North America.

In the US, dollar traveller's cheques are virtually as good as cash in shops and restaurants. But else where you may find some problems. You will probably have to go to a bank to cash a traveller's cheque, where you are likely to be charged a relatively steep commission.(so cash several cheques together, rather than a small amount) Even some banks may not accept your cheque, for fear of forgery and you may well find shops and restaurants especially reluctant. And if your cheques are not in the local currency, you could be hit twice.

OR TRY A LOADED CARD

Cheques of any kind are less widely used nowadays. If people want money, they use a card - and this also applies when you go abroad.(see the chapter on credit cards)The loaded, or prepaid, card has become the present-day traveller's cheque. In the UK you load the card with dollars or euros, by cash on the phone or over the net. When you are abroad, you can readily use your card in the shops(no problem as many are Visa or Mastercard) and go to an ATM when you want cash.

You cannot run up a debt on a loaded card, so you can get a loaded card simply, without going through a bank credit check. You can just spend the amount you have loaded on to the card, but if you run short when abroad you can easily arrange a top-up by phone or net. You can back your currency judgment - load your card with euros when you see what you think is a good exchange rate for the pound.

LOADING IS EASY

Someone else can load money on to your card if they have the details - which is useful when parents want to get money to their backpacking son or daughter strapped for cash on some distant beach. A loaded card gives you a budget, and gives some help on security. At worst, a villain can only steal what is on your card -and you will have that insured. And he cannot use the loaded card to get his hands on your bank balance. If the card is lost or stolen, the supplier just blocks it and sends you a replacement.

Loaded cards are useful, but you need to be aware of costs. Your money will not earn any interest while it is loaded on the card. There may be charges when you make a purchase or draw cash from an ATM, when you give up the card or if you are inactive for a time. You need first to decide what type of card you want - euros only, dollars only or international - and then carefully compare the different cards.

BIGGER DEALS ARE DIFFERENT

Buying foreign currency to go on holiday is familiar to most of us, but for people involved in property abroad the rules are different. More than a million Brits own properties abroad, and many more buy time-shares or rent flats and houses where euros or dollars will be needed. If you are looking at a currency spend of £5,000 or more, you need professional help.

You will need to talk to your bank or go to a foreign exchange broker - some UK stock exchange brokers, including discount brokers, offer clients a foreign exchange service. Suppose, for example, you are buying a holiday flat in Portugal; completion is delayed by red tape, and you want to be sure that you will not have to pay a higher sterling price if the euro jumps in the meantime. You need a futures foreign exchange contract.

There are two basic pieces of jargon:

SPOT DEAL: this is where the money is moved immediately between the UK and abroad, and the equivalent amount is fixed by the exchange rate which operates on the day.

FUTURES CONTRACT: this is an agreement for the future delivery of currency(or any asset)at a predetermined price on a pre-determined date.(For centuries farmers throughout the world have sold their crops through futures deals) A futures contract gives you certainty on what your deal will amount to in pounds sterling.

If you are involved in bigger deals, you will need to learn a new vocabulary. The size of the deal is a lot; a unit is one piece of currency, such as one pound. Some deal types have their own nicknames. Dollar/sterling is called cable - from the old days when quotes went by cable between London and New York.

If you are involved in frequent currency deals, either through property or going on holiday, you should think of starting an account with an overseas bank or asking your own high street bank to open a foreign exchange account.(you will get the rate of interest which applies to the particular currency). This will give you a cushion against changes in exchange rates, and should simplify the procedures of frequent exchange movements.

****

Chapter 6

Half a Dozen Ways To Save Tax

We are all paying more tax. Many households will be hundreds of pounds worse off this year, with better-off families hit the hardest. No less than 45 tax and benefit changes, almost all of them hitting our pockets, took effect last April. The average loss to families is reckoned at £200 a year, coming on top of a £680 loss after changes last January, which included the rise in VAT.

Putting off paying what you owe the taxman - as a million people do every year - is not a remedy. The penalties for missing tax deadlines have been made much tougher since last April. Taxpayers who are in self-assessment will be hit by the new penalties even if no tax is due, but their form is late.

Paying more tax may be inevitable - paying too much is something you should definitely avoid. So here are half a dozen ways to save tax.

1. CHECK YOUR TAX CODE

Look carefully at the coding notice which you will receive in the early months of the year. There is a strong chance that it will be wrong - thanks to the taxman's computer problems over the past few years. The official Public Accounts Committee reported that up to 22 million people had not been taxed accurately since2004-5. That represents more than half of all taxpayers in the UK, so a good chance that this will include you and me!

Check the coding notice against the accompanying notes. Now that interest rates have fallen, make sure that the taxman does not over-state your income from dividends and interest. Some types of people seem error-prone, such as students and mothers who work part-time. When you change jobs, be sure that you get form P45 and give this to your new employer - otherwise you could be put on the wrong coding and pay too much tax.

Check carefully when there is a change in your tax position. Your coding should change in your favour if you give up your company car or trade down to a smaller or greener model.

Pensioners need to be especially vigilant. They should get tax breaks when they reach 65 and then 75 - but check to be sure. Checking is especially important in this tax year, 2011-12, when allowances are changing: the personal allowance goes up to £7,475 and to £10,090 for people aged 75 and above. Marriage allowance is also being increased.

But remember that these allowances start to be reduced once the pensioner's earnings reach £24,000, which represents a small increase over 2010-11. A pensioner is always sure to get the basic personal allowance, now £7,475 - unless they are one of the better-off with a six-figure income. Personal allowances disappear altogether once your income gets much past £100,000. Next year, from April 2012, the tax-free personal allowance for under-65s will be raised to £8,105, The basic rate income tax limit will reduce to £34,370.

2. USE YOUR ALLOWANCES

In many households, the partners often pay different rates of tax - a traditional picture is the husband who draws an executive salary, while his partner stays at home looking after the young children, so paying little tax or maybe no tax at all. There is a simple, tax-reducing rule: the partner with the low tax rate gets the dividend and interest income; the partner with the high tax rate makes the donations to charity. This rule is reckoned to be one of the most important underused ways for people to keep down their tax bills.

Moving the ownership of bank deposits does not raise any tax issues. Moving shares comes free of CGT between a married couple and civil partners, but not to unmarried partners will have to do some tax planning.

Changing the ownership of assets can raise other(non-financial) issues, so there is always the compromise of joint ownership. The Revenue will assume that this means a 50-50 split, but you can arrange to divide differently - and remember to tell the taxman.

Joint ownership also plays a useful role in keeping down Capital Gains Tax(see the chapter on CGT).You can double the amount of gain you can make free of CGT every year to £21,200 from £10,600. When you make gains which do pay tax, the lower tax-paying partner will probably pay 18% while the higher-paid partner will be hit for 28%.

Making payments to charity is exactly the other side of the coin: all payments which are tax-deductible should be made by the partner who has the heavier tax bill. There is a real danger here that one of you will end up paying too much tax. When a charity receives a donation, it can claim tax back from the Revenue.

But if the person making the donation pays little or no tax, and cannot cover the amount the taxman repays to the charity, the Revenue will come on to them for the difference!

This is why charities will often ask you, when you make a gift aid donation, to confirm that you pay sufficient tax to cover their reclaim.

3. £4,250 RENT FREE OF TAX

If you let a furnished room in your house or flat to a lodger, the first £4,250 a year, just over £80 a week, comes free of tax under the Rent-a-Room scheme. The room has to be in the main place where you live, though you do not have to be the owner - you, too, can be a tenant.(If your fellow-tenants in the same property also go in for Rent-a-Room, you will all get an allowance of £2,125 each) The Rent-a-Room scheme was meant to increase the amount of residential property available on the market, so you will not be given the concession if you let to a company for use as office space. And you have to be living in the property, so you will not be able to claim the relief if you move.

When you own the building where the room is let, you will not lose the valuable exemption from capital gains tax when you come to sell - so long as you have just one lodger. The taxman has always been prepared to ignore just one lodger, but two or more means, in his view, that you are running a business.

Rent-a-Room is simple to operate: you log the income and ignore the expenses. If the rent is more than £4,250 a year(this will depend on location)you have a choice. You can pay tax on the excess over £4,250 or you can offset expenses against your income and pay tax on the surplus.

Suppose that you let a room for £7,000 a year; under Rent-a-Room you would pay tax on £2,750, which is the excess over £4,250. If your expenses amounted to £4,000, under the alternative route you would pay tax on the surplus of £3,000 - which is marginally a less attractive deal.

4. DANGER - TAX ON A MODEST INCOME

A large trap lies in wait for people, many of them pensioners, who have a modest income - just a little more than their tax allowances. Typically, these people will draw the state pension, maybe a pension from their former job, and get a small amount of interest from a bank or building society. If all this amounts to less than their tax allowances, they pay no tax: they can get a R85 form from the bank, so that all interest will be paid to them gross. The problem arises when their income is more, even just a little more, than their tax allowances.

A pensioner who has a taxable income, even a small amount, cannot complete a R85 form to have interest paid to them before tax. That means that the bank will send them interest after deducting tax at 20%, as the banks are obliged to do on all interest payments. But that may represent a higher rate than the pensioner should pay. If the pensioner does nothing more, he will have overpaid tax - which is what the experts believe happens to a large number of people. To get the overpayment back from the taxman, the pensioner will have to fill in a self-assessment form and send in a return.

That may look excessive, but tax overpayments can add up over the years to make the claw-back more appealing. And at present there does not seem to be any simple alternative.

5. GOOD IDEA - SACRIFICE YOUR SALARY

Imagine, just for a moment, that you agreed to reduce your salary. You would pay less income tax and National Insurance. Your employer would have a smaller wage bill and he would also pay less NI. The amount saved by you and your employer together could amount to a sizeable total, which could be put to good use.

In this case, the aim is to maintain your net position(after tax and NI) but give you some extra benefits. you agree to a reduction in your cash income in return for non-cash benefits. This is the theory of salary sacrifice, which is offered to employees by a number of major companies.

The most common benefit under salary sacrifice schemes is an improved pension contribution from the employer. Before then, he would simply deduct an employee's pension contribution from his after-tax pay and pass the contributions on to an insurance company. Childcare vouchers are included in some schemes (up to £1,456 in 2011-12) but the range of tax-efficient benefits can be as large as employers and employees choose.

Salary sacrifice schemes include bikes for work, workplace parking and even holiday buying. One water company brought in a scheme which enabled employees to pay their water bills; another scheme offered to provide company cars to people who would not otherwise be eligible.

This financial year, national insurance has been increased again, and more people will have to pay higher-rate tax. Think about salary sacrifice if your salary is around a tax threshold. If you earn £43,475 you would have avoided higher rate tax last year, but in 2011-12 you would have £1,000 taxed at 40% as the threshold drops. To avoid this, you could agree a £1,000 salary sacrifice - you would go back to paying only standard rate tax and your employer could put the £1,000 into your pension pot.

6. GIVE TO CHARITY - THE PROPER WAY

We all like to give to charity, but the experts say that large sums are being lost because we do not all give in a tax-efficient manner. We should all use the Gift Aid scheme, or payroll giving where an employer takes the donation from the employee's wages and hands it over to the charity. Gift Aid payments are set against your taxable income and so reduce your tax bill.

When you donate money to a charity under Gift Aid, this is treated by the taxman as a payment from which basic rate tax of 20% has already been deducted. The charity can reclaim this tax, so long as you, the donor, pay sufficient tax to cover the amount the taxman hands back to them. If you pay tax at 40% or 50%, you can get further relief through self-assessment.

Charities' life was made easier in the budget last March: smaller donations up to £5,000 a year will qualify for Gift Aid without the giver or the charity having to fill out laborious forms. This is great for charities, but you the taxpayer need to make sure that you get tax relief whenever you give to a charity. No one wants to go through a heavy procedure when they put a pound into a collecting tin - but no one wants to miss out on the tax relief.

There is a compromise: a bank-type charity such as the Charities Aid Foundation. Here, you have an account where you get tax relief on the money you pay in. You are given a cheque book, or a card, which you can use to send payments to charities - and you know that the cheques you send will be tax-efficient.

The money you pay in is grossed up for tax in your account, and the charity bank makes a small charge for the operation. You will not receive interest on your account.

If you give shares or property to a charity rather than cash, there is one simple rule: hand over the assets direct, do not cash them in first.(if the shares are not listed, you may need to agree values with the Revenue) If you cash in, you could face a bill for CGT, or help to push other disposals into the CGT-paying zone. Going direct is simpler and tax-effective.

AND FOR SOPHISTICATED RISK-TAKERS......

Investing in small companies, through the Enterprise Investment Scheme or Venture Capital Trusts, is for sophisticated investors who are ready to take some risk. There are tax breaks, which were made bigger in last March's budget. Investment in EIS brings help on capital gains tax(see the CGT chapter)while income tax relief has been raised to 30%. Next year, the rules will be relaxed for the size of companies in which EIS and VCT can invest - and the amount of investment a qualifying company can accept.

****

Chapter 7

How To Handle Your Mortgage

The number of mortgages available has more than doubled over the past two years but the number of approvals continues to fall. Credit crunch made lenders shy away from risk, wiping out 100% mortgages - and Northern Rock's famous 125% Loan to Value - but 85% and 90% mortgages are back in the marketplace. So what is the problem?

The problem is credit scoring. This the same points-based system which is used for credit card applications, except that for mortgages the figures are that much larger. Lenders have been pressured to explain why they refuse applications and to describe the methods they use to assess risks. Each lender has his own methods of calculation and lenders do not make the details public. They do not have to give reasons if they turn you down, nor do they have to explain the minimum score you need. Lenders claim that giving out information of this sort would show fraudsters how to beat the system. In general terms, you can see what lenders are looking for. They want a picture of stability, with evidence that you know how to handle money. This points to a flat or house which you own, a job where you have been working for some years - and no county court judgments.

LONGER TO SAVE

Saving in order to buy a home has become that much harder since the crunch. Earlier this year, building society analysis showed that the average deposit had more than doubled, to 21% from 10%.

With the typical home selling at £161,000, this points to a cash deposit of nearly £35,000.

Even assuming a high savings rate, it was estimated that it now costs the average worker no less than eight years to afford the deposit on an average house.

MAYBE A BROKER

Before you go to a lender and make your score, you need to take some important preparatory steps. First, decide whether or not you want to use a mortgage broker. The broker should know the big picture on mortgages across the UK - or at least parts of it - and a broker will be essential if you are a marginal applicant or if you encounter problems while negotiating with a lender.

At an early stage, you should ask for your credit report. There are three major credit reporting agencies in the UK, and they will send you a copy of your report for a few pounds. The lender will look at your report as a matter of routine, so you should get there first. This becomes extremely important if there is an error in your credit report. You have the legal right to ensure that any errors are corrected, and you need to do so as a matter or urgency.

GO INDEPENDENT?

There is one feature of your credit report which you need to resolve before a lender goes through it. Your report will list anyone with whom you have a joint account - these people are regarded as your financial associates.

Lenders may look at the financial records of these people when you apply for a loan. If they have a poor credit history, your application could be in trouble. You may need help from a credit agency to leave your former joint arrangements and demonstrate that you are independent.

SHOP AROUND - WITH CARE

You will probably want to shop around among lenders to get the best terms, but you need to be aware of a possible problem - the impact on your credit file. Your initial move will be to ask the lender for a decision in principle, which will tell you how much he is prepared to lend. To give you his answer, the lender may run a full credit search.

A full search will leave a trace on your credit file, which could damage your chances of getting a mortgage if you make a number of applications. When a lender sees several application searches over a short period, he may assume that you are desperate for money, maybe over-extended or even that there is identity fraud.

To avoid that, you need to ask the lender to make a .quotation search' at that initial stage - which should not impact on your future applications for credit.

BE 100% ACCURATE

When making your application, this is a time when you need to be 100% accurate. The lender will have your credit report, so that any discrepancies are bad news. If you later realise, say that your initials have been miss spelt on the application, that could have sent the lender away on a credit search for the wrong person. In these sensitive financial times, this may even make him decide to back off.

So you are ready to check out your points on the lender's credit score. It would be a good idea to look in detail at a typical credit score test, work out what the questions involve and then see how you could improve your score. Here are likely questions:

§Age? You may score more if you are over 30.

§Marital Status? Being married or in a civil partnership could score better than being single.

§Children? Negative on grounds of affordability. Lenders vary on how much they reduce the mortgage for the first child - a second child will significantly cut into your scope for borrowing.

§Residence? A house probably better than a flat - though that depends on which part of the UK you live in - and ownership may be better than renting.

§Post Code? A simple question, but could be significant. Discrimination by post code is often raised in education and the NHS; in a mortgage, a .good' post code could be useful though a .bad' one might be neutral.

§How long have you been at your address? The point of the question is clear: in principle, the longer the better. A year is probably the minimum.

§Telephone Number? Maybe not as simple as it looks - the lender could prefer you to have a landline rather than just a mobile.

§Annual Income? Another obvious question, but be ready to provide written back-up for your answer.

§How much do you want to borrow on mortgage? One of the basic issues, which will have been resolved before you see the application form.

§How much deposit do you have? Same as above.

§Over how many years do you wish to repay your mortgage? Same as above.

§How do you want to repay your mortgage? The basic choice here is a repayment mortgage or interest-only. If you choose interest-only, the lender will want to know how he will get his money back.

§How long with your employer? Obvious again, but be certain that your answer is precisely correct and you have written back-up.(talk to your HR department)

§How long with your bank? Check with your bank to make sure, once again, that your answer is precisely correct.

§How many credit cards? Just be sure that you give the right answer - your credit report will provide confirmation.

§Credit limit? This refers to your credit cards and any loans you may have but does not include mortgages. The lender will match this against your income and your outstanding debt.

§Credit outstanding? This means cards and loans; your answer has to be an estimate, but get it as right as you can.(check your current credit card debt by phone or on the net)

§Current/cheque account? This should be simple confirmation.

§County Court judgments? The lender will know the answer from checking your credit file, but he wants to hear it from you.

§Credit account operation? What the lender would probably like to hear is .I never miss a payment.' As he knows your credit file, you have to tell it as it is.

After all this, your application succeeds and the lender gives you your loan. Great, but you look ahead - you will need larger loans over the years to come as your family grows and your earnings progress. So you need to improve and protect your credit score. How do you do that?

Here are six do's and don'ts:

DO make sure that you are on the electoral register. Some lenders will even reject applicants who are not registered: this is regarded as evidence of stability and commitment, and highly regarded by lenders.

Registering is no big deal, and is open to any British citizen(and EU citizens) age 18.

There is a full version, whose use is controlled - it is open to credit reference agencies - and an edited version, which excludes people who have chosen to opt out. Even the full version includes only basic information: name and address, date of birth together with voting information such as your voting number, whether you asked for a postal vote and whether you voted at the last election. If any of this bothers you, register and then opt out.

DON'T close down unused accounts or reduce card limits before you make an application. This is a mistake many people make, and it is actually hurtful - it reduces your credit score. The lender will look at your credit rating in the form of your debt as a percentage of your credit limit.

This means that if you just reduce your credit limit, without paying down any debt, your debt percentage will actually go up! This is the opposite of what you want. It makes sense to run down and close unused accounts, but do so only as your outstanding debt reduces. If you have a 50-50 ratio of debt to credit limit, try to keep to that.

DO monitor your credit file. Ask for a copy every six months, and always ask for a copy shortly after you move house: letters carrying your personal finance details may go astray and get in the hands of a crook.

You can arrange to receive an e-mail alert whenever there is a change to your credit file. Most of these changes will be routine - a company cancels a card which is time-expired - but you need to stay on the lookout for a change which matters.

DON'T miss any loan or card payments, and do not be late. This means that you have to set up direct debits with your bank(where the monthly amounts varies)and standing orders.(where the amount is fixed) Missed and late payments can cause a lot of grief, especially to your credit rating. It is even better, with all bills, to pay early rather than be late. Lenders, in particular, do not like it.

DO have a spread of different types of account - you will have a current bank account, credit cards and your mortgage. Think about adding an overdraft and maybe a personal loan. All this will give you useful flexibility and show the lender you can handle different asset types. Think about it: if you were told nowadays that someone did not have a credit card, you would probably assume that they had been rejected!

DON'T open a number of new accounts at around the same time. For credit cards, the conventional wisdom is not to take out more than two new cards in a six month period. Lenders would think that you were suddenly short of cash or that a scam was taking place. A sudden series of applications(with the later ones likely to be refused) would not look good in your credit report.

DO keep open your accounts which show a good management record, even if they are not being used. For credit scoring it is important to have a history of good account handling - though that does not mean you should accept all the cards which you will be offered.(Take care when you offered apparently attractive preselected or pre-approved cards) Six cards is probably a sensible maximum: general purpose, cash back, overseas, a backup and maybe cards you can use at the supermarket and a petrol station.

READ THE SMALL PRINT

Probably the best advice of all is to buy yourself a magnifying-glass. You will then be able to read the small print of your card or loan terms and conditions. On loans and mortgages, issues can arise over repayment, i.e. when you want to re-mortgage in order to save money on the interest you are paying.

Some credit cards may insist that you spend a certain minimum amount every year; others may charge you if you do not use the card for a period. If you are attracted by cash back card, make sure you know what types of deal will bring you the benefit and when the cash will arrive.

All the time you are building a picture of the perfect borrower - successful, hardworking, reliable, never late. Thanks to credit scoring: you have created a new you!

****

Chapter 8

CGT: Tax When You Sell

Whenever you sell something which has some value, or give it away, you could be facing Capital Gains Tax. (CGT) For the average family, there are three exceptions - the house you live in(your .principal residence'),your car and personal belongings worth up to £6,000. If you hold ISAs and government stock, any gains will also be free from CGT.

But selling your second home at a profit will bring a bill for CGT; so will selling shares and unit trusts. A gift is treated as a sale at the prevailing market price. When making a sale, you can offset costs - such as paying an estate agent to sell your second home. Losses will also reduce your gain(these can be carried forward)though only on assets which rank for CGT. So if you lose money on government stocks or on a stocks and shares ISA, the taxman does not wish to know.

As a further help, there is a annual exemption which is set at £10,600 for 2011-12. If your gains come out at less than this figure, after allowing for any losses and the costs of making the gains, then you will have no CGT to pay. But this exemption is only good for a year at a time - there is no carry forward.(and the figure may be raised, usually only slightly, from one budget to another)

BUSINESS OWNERS BENEFIT

For business owners, there is a special deal known as Entrepreneurs' relief.' This allows them to pay only an effective 10% gains tax on "material" business disposals of shares or assets up to a lifetime limit of £10 million - subject to a number of detailed conditions.

How much CGT you pay was made complex in last year's budget: since June 2010 the CGT rate is 18% for basic rate taxpayers, rising to 28% for higher-rate payers. The Chancellor emphasised that half the people paying CGT are basic rate tax payers - but many of these may have a shock, because there is a quirk in the way the system works.

ADD GAINS TO INCOME

If you make a capital gain, the taxman now adds the amount of the gain to your pre-tax income - and that determines whether you pay 18% or 28%. This means that a basic rate taxpayer who makes a sizable gain - say by selling a holiday flat - will have to pay the higher rate of 28%. This is a significant difference, which comes hard on people who own lumpy assets, such as a second home, which they cannot sell off in small parcels in order to stay within the annual limits.

Probably the only basic rate taxpayers who pay 18% will be people making relatively small gains from dealing on the stock market. You have to remember that since last April the 40% income tax rate kicks in at£35,001,down from £37,401 in 2010-11, which means that another 650,000 people have been paying higher-rate tax. And the personal allowance disappears just under £120,000.

HOW TO PAY LESS

So how do you pay less CGT? The first step is to recognise that no CGT arises when assets are transferred between spouses or civil partners who are living together. If you give shares to your spouse, this is treated as a no gain/no loss transaction, and your spouse takes over the original cost. So you can move assets into joint ownership without any tax come-back, and that immediately doubles your annual tax-free exemption from £10,600 to £21,200.

But remember also that CGT will arise if assets are transferred between partners who are not married or between parents and children. The taxman will also pounce if assets are sold cheaply which could give you a loss - deals have to be done at market value.

USE YOUR EXEMPTION

The second way to keep down the CGT bill is to use your annual exemption. If you do not use it, it is simply lost. You have to be pro-active: suppose that some years ago you bought a parcel of shares which have now rocketed in value.

If you sold the shares, there would be a CGT bill: so you put the shares into joint names, and then sell just enough each year that the gain comes out below the annual exemption level. When this operation is complete, you will own a parcel of shares valued at today's - rather than the original -prices, so that if you come to sell your CGT liability will be that much less. You have to do the math each time. At a gain of£10,500, you are tax-free; with a gain of £10,900, you could start paying 28%.

BED AND BREAKFAST'

You may be unwilling to sell the shares and want to buy them back once you have used up your tax-free exemption for the year. This is known as .bed and breakfast' which used to be extremely popular until the taxman clamped down a few years ago.

Now, the rule is that 30 days must elapse between your selling and your buying back: if you fail the test, the deals will just be ignored for CGT, so that your tax-saving plan would have failed. Markets can move in much less than 30 days, so you have two options. One is for your partner to buy the shares. The second option is for you to choose similar shares - if you had been selling tracker units, buy a tracker from another manager. Getting your partner to buy the shares which you sell is called .bed and spouse.' Another effective plan is known as 'bed and ISA.' You sell your shares, paying any CGT, and use the proceeds to buy them back straightaway into a stocks and shares ISA.(A direct switch is not permitted).

EIS TO HELP

Enterprise Investment Schemes are best known as a way of reducing income tax, but they can also be used to defer CGT liabilities. And a liability deferred is a liability reduced. Growth in the EIS itself is CGT-free provided the shares have been held for three years. More appealing is that you can defer any gain made in the past three years by re-investing into an EIS - and if you have already paid CGT, you can get that back. You can also defer a gain made up to a year after a EIS investment.

Unless the rules change, an EIS investor could continue to defer his capital gains until his death - and there is no CGT when you die. But remember that you will become liable for CGT if you sell the EIS, or if you choose to go non-resident.

NO CGT ON YOUR HOME

For most of us, the big amounts of CGT will be involved when we put property on the market. Your principal residence is free from CGT. This is probably the most important aspect of gains tax for many people: if you have lived in your home and it has been your only home all the time you owned it, then your profit from the sale will come tax-free.

But there are some snags. The taxman will show an interest if you have a very large garden or grounds or extensive outbuildings. More relevant, for most people, is that you will pay tax if any part of the house has been used entirely for business - especially important if you are self-employed. This means that if you seta side a room as study or workroom, you may end up paying CGT. The answer, when you work from home, is to use different rooms from time to time and not to specify any particular part of your house or flat.

YOU HAVE TO CHOOSE

People who are married or in a civil partnership are allowed just one principal residence: when you nominate a property as your main home you have to live there, not just own it. Often, each of the partners previously owned a house. In that case, you have two years in which to send the taxman a jointly signed statement nominating your principal residence. If you do not tell him, he will decide on the facts.

Partners who are not married or in a civil partnership are better off - a rarity in the tax system! Just because they have no formal connexion in the eyes of the taxman, each of them can own a principal residence. This has a clear appeal as the eventual profit on the sale will come tax-free.

But remember: if you let the house which you are not using, or just some of the rooms, you will face a bill for CGT.

A SECOND HOME PAYS CGT

Selling your home comes free from CGT, but selling a home or holiday flat pays the full rate of tax - which is almost certain to be 28%. The most tax-effective move, when people retire, is to sell the main residence and go to live in the former second home, which now becomes the principal residence: the entire deal is free from CGT.

If selling prices were low, some people would let their former main residence, but that needs very careful calculation. You pay CGT when you sell(your old main residence has become your second home) and you could have an income tax bill on your net rental income, after allowing for expenses.

SWITCHING CAN HELP

You decide that you do not want to retire to your second home or holiday flat - you want to sell. You are likely to pay CGT if you have owned the property for any length of time; so what can you do? The short answer is you switch.

Switching - also known as .flipping' -simply means that you change the election on your main residence so that your second home becomes your main residence. After a short period, say just a couple of weeks, you change the election back again. This technique has been widely used by MPs, including the Chancellor in the last Labour government.

THREE YEARS FREE

Because your second home has been your main residence, even for a very short time, the gain which arises from the last three years of ownership comes free from CGT. There is a cost: if you come to sell your main residence, the two weeks when it had ceased to be your main home will fall subject to CGT.

You need to do the calculation before you commit, but three tax-free years in return for two taxable weeks represents a starting ratio in your favour of 78:1. At the least, it is worth checking out the numbers.

MAYBE A HOLIDAY LET

Many people have helped to pay their tax bills by turning their second home into a furnished holiday let - but here again the taxman is tightening the rules. Since last April, you have not been allowed to offset a loss on the holiday let against your other income. Losses can only be set against income from other holiday lets.

From April next year, it will be harder to qualify as a holiday let. Properties will have to be available for 210 days a year and let for at least 105 days. And there is still the rule that lets must be no longer than 31 days.

28% VERSUS 50%

One plus point for CGT is that it hurts less than income tax. The 18/28% rate is higher than 20% standard rate, but less than 40% higher rate(which since last April kicks in at £35,000 a year)and well below the additional rate of 50%.

The message is clear: if your income comes as capital rather than income, your tax bill will be that much less. £100 gross subject to CGT may be worth £82 and no less than £72. £100 pre-tax income to a standard rate taxpayer is worth £80, to a higher rate payer £60 and a top rate payer this financial year just £50. These are significant differences.

The taxman has also done these sums, so there are careful anti-avoidance regulations in place to stop taxpayers rushing to turn income into capital. But there are some types of assets where the return comes as capital - and so relatively lightly taxed - rather than as income or a mixture of income and capital.

HOW ABOUT A ZERO?

Probably the best-known producers of capital but no income are zero-dividend preference shares, which you can buy direct or through a unit trust. Zeros are issued by investment trusts, and they do what it says on the tin: you are simply promised that your shares will be repaid at a certain price at a certain date in the future. You then do some math and work out the effective yield you are being offered.

Zeros are not risk-free. A few years back, a number of companies got into problems because they had borrowed from the banks and/or had been buying each others' shares. If zeros appeal to you, choose one that has been issued by a major financial group or one where you can see from the published data that the trust's assets are already sufficient to meet the repayment. Zeros are listed, so you can sell without having to wait for repayment; the zero unit trusts will not have a maturity date.

OR PERHAPS A DRP?

A Defined Return Plan is designed for investors who are looking for predictable returns - and are prepared to accept some capital risk in exchange for an appealing potential reward. All of the returns are taxed as capital gains, so that buyers can use their annual exemption or carried-forward losses. DRPs can even be put into an ISA, making all the return tax-free.

A typical DRP works like this: you get a fixed return after, say, three years provided that the stock market index has not fallen below its starting level. If that works, you get 7.25% multiplied by the number of years the plan has been in force. That represents an appealing return by the standards of early 2011, but the investment is not risk-free.

You can start to lose capital if the stock market crashes - specifically if the index closes more than 50% below its starting level. If that happens, your capital will be reduced on a 1:1 basis in line with the index. The time to start a DRP has to be when the stock market is low, or at least when there will not be another 2007-8 crunch. Be aware that the minimum investment may be £5,000 or more and you should regard the money as locked away - perhaps available in the interim, but at a penalty. If all works, a tax-free 7.25% carries a lot of appeal.

OR MAYBE THE US GOVERNMENT

Zero-coupon bonds are safer than zero-coupon preference shares, as their security is stronger - but these do not exist within the UK. You have to go to the eurodollar market, but this is essentially for professional operators. A bigger market operates on Wall Street in US Treasury bonds. Interest rates are comparable to the UK, and you also have a currency risk - or benefit.

If you think about a 10-year Treasury bond, it consists of two things: (1)20 interest payments, i.e. one every six months fixed for 10 years, and (2) repayment of the principal, which takes place when the bond matures in 10 years' time. The stock market then turns (1) and (2) into separate securities.

Investors who want assured income or do not pay tax - such as pension funds and charities - will buy the bond which gives them the stream of income. People who prefer to receive a capital profit will prefer the bond which gives them the right to repayment when the original matures.

TAX IN A TAKE-OVER

All these ideas are based on the assumption that you can control, at least to some extent, when and how to make capital gains. But there is one important area where you can suddenly find you are facing a capital gain which you did not arrange - when you hold shares in a company which is taken over. A handsome capital gain may be just the problem you would like to have; but as you cannot control the timing, you need to reflect in advance how you are going to react.

You may read the first news in the newspapers that your shares are being bid for and that the directors support the deal. You will then be sent a copy of their press statement; within a few weeks(up to four) you will get a hefty document which is the formal offer for the shares you own. From then on, the clock is running.

You should have several weeks - three weeks is the minimum - in which to decide what to do.

TAX-FREE SHARE SWAPS

Some take-overs, especially if they come within the UK, involve an exchange of shares. That does not raise any immediate CGT issues. Instead of owning 100 shares in company A, you now own 120 shares in company B. The date and cost of acquisition remain the same.

CGT will arise if the take-over bid is made in cash, or a mixture of shares and cash.(You will also pay CGT if you do not like the look of the bidding company and decide to sell your shares in the stock market)Then you may be facing a tax bill you did not choose and probably do not want!

THINK STOCK TRANSFER

When a take-over involving cash is announced, the first thing you should do is make sure that the shares are held in the joint names of yourself and your partner. This will double the amount of gain which you can make free of CGT, to £21,200 from £10,600. If you have not already done that, contact the company registrar or (which would be quicker)download a stock transfer form on the net.

Some take-overs involve a mixture of shares and cash. These generally offer a .mix and match. facility which allows shareholders some freedom of choice as to which they would prefer.(pension funds, which do not pay tax, may choose cash while private shareholders facing CGT bills will prefer shares)

If after all this you are still looking at a CGT bill, check around to see if you have shares or other assets which you could sell at a loss. If you finally have to pay CGT, you can always reflect that 18/28% still means less to pay than income tax at 40/50%.

****

Chapter 9

Getting Cash Out of Your House

You are retired; you have debts, you would like to help your children buy a house, you would like a holiday. You are .asset rich, cash poor.' Your house is your major asset - how do you get your hands on some cash?

The traditional answer was to downsize: your children no longer live at home, so your house is too big for you and your partner. You could move to a smaller house or flat, perhaps sheltered housing, and you will release some tax-free cash from the sale of your home. And when you downsize you get the full market value for your house.

But there are problems with downsizing. You may like the house and the area where you live, and to find a smaller, much cheaper, home may mean moving to another part of the country. Moving home is a hassle, and it costs: you will be paying an estate agent, a lawyer and a removal firm. Biggest spend of all, you will be paying stamp duty on your new house or flat - if it costs £300,000, stamp duty will add £9,000. This is why the average cost of a house move in the UK now runs into five figures.

REALISE VALUE

So you think equity release, which means what it says on the tin. You realise some of the value in your house, i.e. what it is worth over and above any mortgage or borrowing. You do not have to move house and you will not have any interest or similar payments to make. The minimum age for equity release is usually set at 55(the younger of you and your partner) though older people get better terms.

Most homes in England and Wales will be eligible, assuming that they are worth at least £75,000 and are not of a particularly unusual design.(Some lenders avoid Scotland, where the legal system is different, and only a few cover Northern Ireland)If you still have a mortgage, this will have to be paid off, or netted out as part of the total financing.

LIFETIME MORTGAGE......

There are two types of equity release - a lifetime mortgage and home reversion. Under a lifetime mortgage, you borrow a proportion of your home's value, usually between 25% and 40%. Interest is charged but nothing has to be paid back until you die or sell your home to go into long-term care. The interest is rolled up, or compounded, over the period of the loan. If you live to a very ripe old age the loan will grow substantially: if you pay interest at 5%, the loan will double in 15 years, and at 7% in just 10 years.

The older you are, the better the terms. When this was written, a couple aged 65 living in a £500,000 house would be able to release £165,000. If the same couple were 75, they would be able to raise £215,000.

Virtually all lenders will give you a .no negative equity' guarantee, which means that the amount of the loan will never exceed the value of the house. This gives the comfort that, however long you live and whatever happens to house prices, your home will not involve a debt for your heirs.

.....OR HOME REVERSION

Under a lifetime mortgage, you remain the owner of your house. Under the alternative scheme, home reversion, you sell a share of your property - up to 100%, if you choose - at a discount to its market value. You sign a tenancy agreement, which gives you and your partner the right to stay in your home for the rest of your lives. There may be a nominal rent, and you agree to keep the house insured and in good condition.

When you have both died or gone into long-term care the house is sold and the lender takes his share of the sale price. So if you had originally sold 25% of your property, the lender will take that same proportion of the proceeds. In this way, the lender can share in the price appreciation.

COSTS ARISE

Under both types of scheme, there will be some costs. You may go to a financial adviser, you will need a lawyer and the lender will want an independent valuation of your home as the basis for his loan. There may also be an application fee. Some lenders will pick up part of the legal and valuation fees - maybe add them to your borrowing - which means they will decide which firms you use.

There is a trade body for equity release called SHIP(Safe Home Income Plans) whose members follow a code of conduct - including the .no negative equity' guarantee.

You will be able to move house after taking out equity release, but there may be some restrictions. If you move to a much smaller house, you may have to repay part of your loan.

DECISIONS BEFORE YOU COMMIT

The great appeal of equity release is that you get a piece of cash and there are no outgoings to meet the interest cost. Instead of a lump of cash, you can agree to take your money in instalments, which will keep down the interest charges. But there are some other decisions you need to make before committing to equity release. First, you need to talk to your family. Equity release creates a debt on your house, which is probably your biggest single asset. That will reduce the value of your estate when you die, though it will also bring down the amount of Inheritance Tax which has to be paid.(see comments on IHT)

REMEMBER COMPOUND INTEREST

Under a lifetime mortgage, the loan may grow very large if you or your partner live for another 20-30 years, though you still have your guarantee that it will never exceed the value of the house.(Compound interest is a force to be reckoned with: at 5% interest, a loan of £100,000 will grow to £265,000 after 20 years) .

Under home reversion, you can ensure that some value stays in the family by selling the lender only a part share of your home.

Which type of equity release works best will depend on future house prices. If they rise, you win under a lifetime mortgage by remaining the owner of your home. If house prices are roughly static, or fall, you will be relatively better off under home reversion.

TAX EFFECTS

Secondly, you need to check for unintended consequences. Equity release itself does not carry any tax implications, but there may be consequences when you receive a sizeable cash sum or a series of income payments. These could affect your entitlement to means-tested benefits and grants, from both central and local government. You need to work this out before you sign up.

You also need to consider the knock-on tax effects of whatever you do with the money. Maybe you will give some away(so think IHT)and maybe you will invest some.(so think income tax and ISAs for you both).

You should not have to worry too much about the way equity release schemes are operated. The major players are big insurance companies, and equity release is supervised by the Financial Services Authority. (There are rather fewer lenders in equity release than five years ago, so look around and/or talk to a financial adviser)

LONG-TERM COMMITMENT

You should think carefully about taking out equity release, as this is intended to be a long-term in fact lifetime commitment. If your circumstances change, and you want to repay early, you may find that this will cost. So you need to be pretty sure, if you go ahead, that you will not need to use the equity in your house for any other purpose. You need to work through this scenario with your adviser as well as other possibilities: suppose you and your partner take out a home reversion plan, and you both die within a few years. If that happens, you will have sold an interest in your home(perhaps even a 100% interest)at a significant discount to its market value.

For many people(around 20,000 last year) equity release remains the only ready way to improve their retirement or give meaningful help to the next generation. If you find that inflation is squeezing your retirement income, equity release has to be worth considering.

Chapter 10

You May Need Insurance

Life insurance could be one of the most important things you buy - especially when you buy a house or start a family. Buying life insurance used to be simple, but life insurance has been hit by the European court decision which bans what they call .gender-based pricing.' From December 2012 insurance companies will not be allowed to act on the risk differences between men and women, promising an upheaval in motor insurance and annuities, but also affecting life insurance.

When this was written, the insurance industry was forecasting a 20% rise in life insurance premiums for women and around 10% for men. Women will be hit harder because, as they live longer than men, they paid less under the old set-up.

4X COVER

If you are employed, taking out life insurance may not even be necessary. You need to talk to Human Resources to establish what is available. Many companies offer 4X life cover, which is the maximum the taxman will allow. This means that four times your salary goes to your estate or whoever you nominate.

That level of cover will be enough for some people, maybe not if you have just taken out a large mortgage or if you have children below school age. The basic calculation is that your insurance should cover your debts and set aside sufficient for your partner and children.(for a newly born child, you are looking at a 20-year policy)

And you may be self-employed or you may be worried that the company which employs you may die first!

THINK TERM COVER

To cover a mortgage, term cover represents the most economic form of life insurance. The insurance company agrees to pay out if you die within a pre-agreed term of years. At the end of the period, the policy lapses with no value. One advantage of term insurance is that you can adapt the cover if you take out a repayment mortgage - currently more popular than interest-only. You can take out decreasing term insurance as your monthly repayments of the mortgage loan gradually reduce the amount you have borrowed. If you choose an interest-only mortgage, you will need to keep term cover for the life of the mortgage.

Buying life insurance should be straightforward: you decide how much cover you need for how long and then sign up to the monthly or quarterly premiums. But you need to be aware what will affect how much you pay.

You will pay more if you have risky sports or hobbies, such as diving and mountaineering. Some occupations cost more, notably oil and gas especially for working offshore. (So check if there are specialist insurers who can help) Your medical history will also matter: you will pay extra if you smoke, if you have high blood pressure or if there are health issues in your family history.

NO ANNUAL RENEWAL

Paying for life insurance needs some thought. We are all used to shopping around for insurance, which you will do when you take out life cover. But there is an important difference between life insurance and motor or travel insurance. With life cover, there is no annual renewal, so that people can - and do - go on paying the same premium for years.

This does not make good financial sense. You will need to increase life cover if you re-mortgage or if you have more children. You may be able to reduce the amount of cover - and the premiums - if you give up smoking(to insurance companies, a non-smoker is someone who has not smoked in the previous 12 months.

Growing older might reduce the premiums. If you take out a policy, and your health and lifestyle do not change, you could find that you can cut the premium costs.

It makes sense to review your insurance protection every few years. In particular, you will have to take account of inflation which will steadily reduce the real value of the cover you have arranged. This underlines the case for a periodic review - you could find that your policy comes with indexation or you could choose an .increasing term' policy where the payout is raised by say 5% a year.

NOT JUST PRICE

You will probably find a wide range of charges when you shop around for life cover, but you should not buy life cover just on the basis of price. Life insurance is necessarily complicated and you need to look carefully at the policy coverage and the extras within the cover to make sure that you are getting the best coverage.

Many people find this process complex: if you are in any doubt, take professional advice. Life cover is too important for uncertainty.

Term insurance meets most people's requirements. But some find it hard to accept the notion that they pay insurance premiums for 15 or 20 years, never make a claim, and end up with nothing when they survive. Others prefer to arrange for a sum of money to be paid whenever they die.

WHOLE LIFE COSTS MORE

These kinds of people will choose .whole life' policies. As a payment is guaranteed at some point, whole life policies cost more than term insurance. They combine insurance with investment, which gives you a choice: if you opt for a low level of cover, most of your premiums will be used to build up investments. If you prefer high insurance cover, your premiums will go to life protection rather than investments.

Not so very long ago, many of us would have taken out endowment policies as an alternative to whole life. Endowments guarantee to pay a minimum amount after a certain number of years or if you die in the interim. This minimum amount is increased each year through reversionary bonuses, which cannot be taken back once they have been awarded. Alas, poor stock market performance compelled insurance companies to cut their bonuses - several million homeowners who hoped that endowment policies would pay off their mortgage were sadly disappointed. Endowment policies have become a relatively small market - people who would have paid endowment policy premiums are probably putting their money into ISAs.

COVER THE MAJOR DEBTS

But just what are the risks you need to cope with? Death is the absolute risk, but in Britain today illness or redundancy are more likely to affect the average family. And the average family, as well know, will have two major debts - mortgage and credit card. So two specialist types of insurance have developed.

Mortgage Payment Protection Insurance(MPPI) does what it says: if you lose your job or illness prevents you from working, you will get monthly tax-free payments so that you do not get into mortgage arrears. These benefits will be paid for a limited period, typically two years - and MPPI will probably not help if you gave up your job voluntarily.

MPPI/PPI

People alleged miss-selling of PPI - that it was sold by high pressure tactics to those who did not need it, that it was slipped unreproted into financial packages and that there were high rejection rates on claims. Borrowers were sometimes told, wrongly, that payment protection Insurance was necessary if they wanted a loan. PPI looked sensible (it is sometimes called loan protection) as payment protection was meant to help if you lost your job and could not keep up monthly payments on credit cards and loans.

The banks have given way to all these criticisms of PPI and set aside seriously large amounts of cash to compensate people who were charged the premiums. payment protection grew into very big business: on one estimate, there were around 20 million policyholders in the UK with a typical premium equal to a hefty 15% of the loan balance.

Anyone who bought PPI should seek compensation from whoever supplied it. If necessary, you can go to the Financial Ombudsman. Anyone who took out a loan or a credit card should check the small print to see if PPI was included in the package. - if it was go for compensation.

PPI, if you want it, will cover you for accident, illness, unemployment and other unexpected problems. So you should think hard about what exactly it is you want to protect. For many people, the answer has to be: protection against losing your income and against being found to have a serious illness. If you are employed, the first step is to check what your employer will provide if you are off work because of illness or injury. If you are content with your employer's package, your concern will be with unemployment - which comes as an option under income protection.

WHICH COMES FIRST

Some insurance experts will tell you that income protection is the first insurance you should buy - before your life and even before your car! Just work out, they say - especially if you are self-employed with a young family - if your income were to stop for more than a few months.

So you buy income protection: the best, and most expensive, policies will give you a monthly tax-free amount three months after you stop working until your retirement date. The maximum you can buy probably be set at half of your current income. To keep the cost down, you can extend the initial waiting period beyond three months and reduce your retirement age.

ASU PACKAGE

You will probably find that unemployment insurance is not sold as a stand-alone product, but often as part of an ASU package -

accident, sickness, unemployment. Cover for unemployment will probably be set for a year as the maximum and the unemployment must be enforced - voluntary redundancy is unlikely to be covered. Nor will you be covered if you know that your job faces a specific risk: that is the case for taking cover sooner rather than later.

Cost for unemployment cover will depend on timing: there will be an initial 90-120 days after taking out the policy. After that, you have flexibility: you can arrange a policy which starts paying out immediately, or after a delay of up to three months. The shorter the delay, the more you pay.

CRITICAL ILLNESS COVER

Critical illness insurance seems closer to pure insurance - protection against the possible occurrence of an unpleasant event. Some people regard life cover as sufficient but that will pay out only when you die or are diagnosed with an illness which will be terminal within 12 months. Critical illness cover will pay you a tax free lump sum if you are diagnosed to have any of a range of specified illnesses. Cancer, heart attack, stroke form the basics which are covered and some plans also include loss of sight or hearing and permanent disability.

The experts' advice in critical illness cover is - do not buy on price. What matters is to take out a comprehensive policy, because the insurance company will pay out only on the illnesses which are specified. The other piece of advice is: be upfront about your health, both current conditions and your health history. Insurers will tell you that critical illness claims arise far more often than on life policies. If you are less than forthcoming, your risk is that the insurer may turn down your claim.

In insurance, there is no right answer - except with 20-20 hindsight! Which type of insurance policy you choose will depend on your job, your health, your family situation and your medical history. Do your homework, use the net, talk to friends, pay for advice if you are at all uncertain - and always read the small print.

****

Chapter11

How Pensions Can Double Your Money

Pensions are complicated - but you just need to hold on to two essentials. One is that a pension will provide your income when you have stopped working. The second is that, while you are still working, a pension is by far the best way to cut your tax bill.

Forget all the pension wisdom you have learned in past years - the rules changed in a big way from April 2011. The first big change is that you can put all of your salary into a pension, capped at £50,000 a year. If you go over the £50,000 you will have to pay tax at your top rate, but you have two let-outs.

One let-out is that you can go back over the three previous years and offset any of the allowance which you did not use at that time. The second is that you can choose to have the payment made by your workplace pension fund if the bill comes to more than £2,000. The advantage of that route is that you would be paying out of gross, rather than after-tax, income.

FINAL SALARY TRAP

Some really scary news is that the taxman has laid a trap for people who are still in a Final salary (defined benefit) scheme - when they get a salary increase. The trap arises because the taxman sees how much your salary increase is worth in terms of extra pension and sets that figure against your permitted £50,000 a year. And you may not have noticed that, in the small print, the Revenue has raised this .contribution value' from 10 times to 16 times.

Here is the trap in action. Take a man, paid £50,000 a year, who has worked for his employer for 25 years. Assume that he is on a typical 60ths plan(he gets a pension of 1/60 of salary for every year he works)and has a pension currently worth around £21,000 a year. Good news: he is promoted and gets a hand some salary increase. Bad news: he also gets a hefty tax bill on his improved pension.

16X MULTIPLIER

Suppose his new salary has been raised from £50,000 to £60,000, so that his new pension is worth around£25,000 a year, i.e. an extra £4,000. The taxman multiplies this extra by the factor of 16, and tells the previously happy man that the .contribution value' which he has received from his employer is reckoned at £64,000.

That is £14,000 above the annual limit of £50,000, so the taxman sends in a bill. The newly promoted man isa 40% taxpayer, so he finds himself £5,600 worse off - virtually all of his salary increase by now has gone to the taxman. This trap will also apply if someone has a redundancy payment put into their pension.

ANNUITY NOT NEEDED

Final salary schemes are less common today, as employers moved from defined benefit to defined contribution and many people took charge of their own pension pots though SIPPs, self-invested personal pensions. SIPPs, which are widely offered by brokers and insurance companies, give all the advantages of a pension fund. When you pay money in you automatically get 20% tax relief, ie the standard rate. If you pay tax at 40% or 50% you get further relief through your tax return. Your investments grow free of UK income and capital gains tax.

Until last April, you had no choice - you had to use your pension pot to buy an annuity when you reached age

75. That requirement, which goes back many years, has been dropped. Instead, you can set up a drawdown scheme. You can still take 25% as a tax-free lump sum, leaving the rest invested while you draw an income from it. When you die you can pass on your pension pot - this is another change - after a 55% tax charge.

Annuities may no longer be compulsory at age 75, but they could well remain the first choice for many people. You have to compare the different terms on offer, and once bought annuities cannot be changed. But they are safe, and you know what you are going to get. Staying invested through drawdown is riskier - it depends on your investment skills - and probably more suitable for larger pension pots which are better able to cope with risk.

INCOME RULES FOR DRAWDOWN PENSION

Drawdown schemes have rules which govern the amount of income you can take. Since last April you have been given a choice. You can draw the equivalent of what an annuity would provide. As an alternative, you can draw as much as you like from your drawdown provided you can show that you have a guaranteed lifetime income of £20,000 a year.(Presumably, so that if everything goes pear-shaped, you will not be a burden to the social services)

This £20,000 has to be certain - investment income will not do, you need to be able to show money from the state pension, an occupational scheme or an annuity, People attracted by the freedom of drawdown will probably take out an annuity to cover the £20,000 and invest the rest.

SHOP AROUND

If you do choose an annuity, there are two pointers to remember. The first is to shop around, which many people fail to do. The difference between the best and lowest annuity rates offered by insurance companies can be around 30% - which will affect your income for the rest of your life. Shopping around is not difficult: you can go to an adviser(who will get his fee from the insurance company)or you can check it yourself on the net.

The second pointer is to ask whether you qualify for an enhanced annuity. More than 40% of people who retire are entitled to better annuity rates because of health or lifestyle situations. If you or your partner smoke, or have diabetes or high blood pressure, you are likely to qualify.

Which type of annuity you choose is more of a problem. Many people opt for a level annuity, where the amount of money you get is fixed - a level annuity will give you the highest level of current income. You can choose an annuity which is linked to inflation; this will give you a smaller current income, but its real purchasing power will stay the same. As a compromise, you can go for an annuity which has built-in growth, say 2% or 3% a year.

PENSION FROM NO EARNINGS

£50,000 a year now sets the ceiling for pension contributions, but many people do not appreciate that there is no floor - you do not need to have any earnings at all to get tax relief for a pension.(so open to pensioners and people who are not working)

This is sometimes called the stakeholder scheme, where you can invest up to £3,600 a year and get a 20% subsidy. You can set up a plan for anyone you choose, charges are low and you can stop and start with minimum fuss.

£100 WORTH FOR £80

A stakeholder scheme works simply. If you want to contribute the maximum £3,600 you send a cheque for £2,880, after allowing for relief at the standard 20% rate of tax. The taxman then hands over the remaining£720 to the insurance company, which means that you are getting £100 worth of pension assets for just £80.

When you reach age 75, you can cash in 25% of the pot in the usual way - and probably put the rest into an annuity.

This payment from the taxman even goes to people who do not pay tax. You can set up a stakeholder pension for your elderly mother who is outside the tax system or for your partner who has no income while she stays at home to look after the children.

WAY TO SAVE

Tax-deductibility makes pension contributions an extremely powerful way to save - as tax rates rise, more powerful even than an ISA. If you link this to the ability to take 25% cash tax-free, you have the scope to make some impressive returns.

Take the example of a man, aged 65, just about to retire who pays higher-rate 40% tax. He decides to put£10,000 into a pension policy. Look at what happens next:

§ he gets 40% tax relief, so that the £10,000 policy costs him £6,000.

§ he cashes in 25% of the policy, so that he gets £2,500 cash free of tax and the policy is reduced by the same amount, to £7,500 from £10,000.

§ he now has a policy for £7,500 which has cost him £3,500, and for security he decides to buy an annuity.

§ to keep it simple, he opts for an annuity on a single life(just himself) and accepts the best offer for his policy, which is just under 7%.

§ he now has an income of £520 a year, equal to a safe yield of 14.9% on the £3,500 which he has spent. He is getting 30 times the Bank of England's base rate, and five times more than an instant access account.

He thinks that he has been very clever.

LIFETIME LIMIT

The taxman limits the amount you can put into a pension each year - and he imposes another limit, known as the lifetime allowance, when you retire. Since last April, the lifetime allowance has been fixed at £1.5 million. Anything in your pension pot which is above that figure will be taxed at the penal rate of 55%.

In view of the way the Revenue now values pension assets, more people are likely to hit this ceiling. The taxman values your pension pot by taking the tax-free cash lump sum and then adding 20 times your annual pension. One way round is to ring-fence your pension pot. You will not be taxed as its value increases, but in return you have to stop making any further pension contributions.

RETIRE EARLY?

For high earners, there are only two alternatives to paying 55% tax. One is to retire early, so that you accrue smaller pension rights. You will have a lower pension, though you will get it for longer. The second alternative is to take the maximum amount of tax-free cash when you retire - up to 25% of the new lifetime allowance, equal to £375,000.

There is a trade-off between cash and income, which the Revenue has decided is 14:1. This means that you give up £1 of income for every £14 you take as cash. So if a high earner takes £100,000 cash(as opposed to taking all his pot as pension) his income will be reduced by £7,142 a year. As the taxman takes 20 times your pension when he values your pension pot, the capital value of your pension assets will have been reduced by £142,840.

NEST FOR MILLIONS

The biggest change of all to Britain's pensions will come next year, when the government launches Nest (National Employment Savings Trust) - intended to nudge around 5 million of low to moderate earners into saving for a pension. Every employee aged between 22 and the state retirement age who earns more than £5,000 a year will be enrolled, though they will be able to opt out.

After a transitional two years, the aim is that 8% of people's pay between £5,000 and £33,000 will go into the scheme. The employee will provide 4%, the employer 3% and the government 1% though tax relief. While all this is going on, the state pension scheme will also change - the process of raising the retirement age for women started last year, so by 2020 men and women will both retire at age 65.

EARNINGS LINK

One positive change to state pensions is that increases are to be linked to earnings rather than price inflation -good news because earnings have historically risen faster than prices. The government has set the target date for the change-over as next April .subject to affordability.' Experts fear that the start could be delayed, possibly until 2015.

Nest will aim to deliver a pension equal to 15-18% of a typical worker's pay. For an employee on £25,000 that would mean a weekly private pension of around £75 on top of the basic state pension of £97.65. The money will be invested to match the three phases of a member's career - foundation, growth and consolidation.

The money managers seem to be planning a low-risk, low-return strategy. How far this appeals will become clear over the years - as Nest gradually turns into one of the biggest pension funds in the world!

****

Chapter 12

Tax on Your Heirs

There is one good thing you can say about Inheritance Tax (IHT) - the theory is straightforward. On your death, the taxman looks at all your assets round the world, including the former tax-free ISAs, then he takes off what you owe. If the result comes out at less than £325,000, there is no IHT to pay. Anything above that is taxed at 40%.

Transfers between husband and wife or civil partners are free from IHT. By contrast, there are no concessions for partners who are outside these two groups.

FIX TO 2015

This £325,000 is your tax-free allowance.(rather less than the average value of a house in Greater London) At one time, this allowance was supposed to rise each year in line with inflation, but the Coalition has fixed the present figure until 2015. Anything below the annual allowance is known as the .nil-rate band,' which plays an important role in saving on IHT.

Gifts to charities(anywhere in Europe, not just the UK)are exempt from IHT. Last March's budget added a further boost to charity-giving, by cutting the IHT rate by 10% - from 40% to 36% - if 10% of the estate is left to charity. This 10% applies to the net estate, i.e. above the nil rate band and allowing for any exemptions such as donations to political parties.

USE THE ALLOWANCE

The tax-free allowance applies to each person, but the last Labour government brought in a useful benefit. A married couple(or civil partners)can take over any of the IHT allowance which the other one did not use. This is how it works: suppose that in a married couple, the husband dies and leaves everything to his widow. That means there is no IHT to pay - so he has used none of his allowance. The widow takes his unused £325,000, so that when she dies the tax-free allowance on her estate doubles to a useful £650,000.

When there are children, the husband could leave the nil-rate band to them and the rest of his estate to his widow. This means that there is no unused IHT allowance to benefit the widow, but there are two advantages: (1) there will be no IHT to pay on his death, and (2)the total estate will have been reduced by £325,000, which is equal to a tax saving of £130,000.

This topping-up will still work even if the spouse or partner has already died, so long as their death has taken place since March 1972. But anyone who plans to look back over the past near 40 years to claim some unused IHT needs to consider: the taxman will want to see written evidence, not just a death certificate and probate documents, but clear proof of how much IHT was paid.

TAXED TWICE?

Many people resent IHT: they paid tax on their income while building up assets over the years, but when they want to leave something to their children the taxman takes another big bite. This looks as though what they own has been taxed twice. So how do you save on IHT?

The first step is to make a will - which the experts believe that many, maybe most, of us fail to do. (if you do not make a will, you die .intestate')There are two strong reasons for making a will: to make sure that your assets go where you want and to save on IHT. Suppose that you, the husband, wanted to leave everything to your widow, which would have avoided paying any IHT, but you did not get round to making a will. In that case, other relatives may be entitled to a share and that could also mean paying IHT.

If you are in an unmarried partnership - as are several million people in the UK - then making a will is essential. At present, the law does not recognise unmarried partners, unless the one who survives was financially dependent. For unmarried partners, it is important to make a will and to take care over how you designate assets.(To make a will, go to a solicitor; you could save a few pounds on a DIY will but you would have wasted your money if it was later successfully challenged)

GIVE NOW

The simplest, and most logical, way to reduce the IHT bill is to give now - rather than later. All gifts which are made more than seven years before the giver dies come free of IHT. There is some benefit even before the seven years, because the taxman operates a sliding scale: full tax is due on a gift made within three years of death, but the IHT is reduced by 20% for years 3-4, 40% for years 4-5, 60% for years 5-6 and 80% for years 6-7.

To make giving easier, there are certain types of gift which can be made free from IHT. You can give £3,000 a year to anyone you want and you can defer for a year. You can also make any number of small gifts of £250 a year - though not to the same people. The taxman also smiles on parents who want to give money to their children when they marry: each parent can give £5,000 to each adult child. Other relatives can give £2,500 IHT-free, and anyone else can give £1,000.

People who have a significant income, and who make a habit of distributing some of it, can make big reductions in their IHT bills. There is no upper limit on regular gifts out of surplus income, but you have to satisfy three key tests. The gifts must be made out of income, as opposed to selling assets or borrowing; the gifts must be regular, say by paying annual premiums into an insurance policy, and they must not reduce the giver's standard of living. If you want to follow this route, you need to arrange professional advice.

BE AWARE OF TRAPS

OK you say, the key way for most people to reduce IHT is basically simple: you give away what you want, you live for seven years, and you completely escape IHT. Correct, but you need to be aware that there are some dangerous traps for the unwary. The biggest trap is what the taxman calls .a gift with reservation,' by which he means that you reserve some benefit from the gift. You may have made the gift 20 years ago, but if you reserved any benefit, the gift will be ignored: the IHT bill will be calculated as if the gift had never happened.

Suppose that you give a picture to an old friend; he insists that it should stay in your hall so that you can continue to enjoy it. If you agree, you will have lost any IHT benefit. Suppose that you want to give your holiday flat to your daughter and you formally transfer the deeds. Just remember that if you ever use the flat yourself, you must pay your daughter a full economic rent. If you fail to do that, you will have reserved some benefit; for calculating IHT, the transfer was simply a complete non-event.

A further, subtle, trap is the pre-owned assets test.(POAT) This test, which was introduced because people were avoiding gifts with reservation, states that you will pay tax if you benefit from an asset which you previously owned - and the test goes right back to 1986. The law is new and complex, but one expert quotes this example: in the early 1990s, a father gives his young son a small holding of shares. Seven years go by, so there is no IHT; the prices rocket(think Microsoft)so the happy son, in return, puts down the deposit on a retirement flat for his now elderly father. POAT strikes! Father faces a tax bill.

SEND A LETTER

Some of the ways to avoid or reduce IHT may seem complex, but it is important not to forget the basic rules.

When you make a gift of any size, it is a good idea to send a letter to the happy recipient. This could be important if later the taxman - or one of the beneficiaries of your will - raises a query.

When you are investing, remember the IHT advantages of the Alternative Investment Market. Shares on AIM count as unlisted; if you buy shares in an unlisted trading business and hold them for two years, the holding will escape IHT. Remember IHT when you and your family are thinking about equity release(see chapter nine)and most lenders will now give a guarantee that borrowers will never go into negative equity. When you take out equity release, you create a debt which reduces the value of your estate and therefore the amount of IHT. In its simplest form, you could take out equity release and give the cash to your children. If you survive for seven years, there will be no IHT to pay and some benefit after three years.

EIS CAN HELP

Putting money into an Enterprise Investment Scheme generally appeals to people who want to cut the tax bill on their income, or who want to roll over capital gains. But if you go into an EIS, it is also worth remembering that there is some help on IHT. If you have held the EIS for at least two years(and the company is still in business)there is no IHT on the value of your investment.

The EIS simply falls outside the estate for IHT purposes. The hope is that the investment has done well -relief is based on its value at the time of death, as opposed to the original cost.

USING TRUSTS

Some people like to use trusts in their financial affairs, especially to protect future generations and to help ward off problems. Trusts can be used to cut the bill for IHT, but you should remember two obvious points:

you will need to go to a lawyer, and the process will cost. Two types of trust are worth considering: under a Loan Trust you make a small gift to set up the trust, followed by an interest-free loan.(which you could call in if circumstances change)The trustees invest the loan so that all the growth comes outside your estate for IHT.

As a second choice, you could create a discretionary trust which should cost only a few hundred pounds to set up. You can shelter assets of £325,000 per person, or £650,000 for a married couple or civil partners, and there will be no IHT so long as you, the donor, survive for seven years. The trust will typically have two trustees, often the parents who are giving money to their children. This equates to making a gift - but with the crucial difference that the donor can keep control of the assets.

CHANGE YOUR LIFESTYLE?

Saving money on IHT, as with most tax planning, depends on your lifestyle and how far your are prepared to change. Some financial advisers, when asked about IHT saving, used to say "Become a gentleman farmer."

The rules governing agricultural land relief are highly complex, but as a general rule agricultural land which is let out can become IHT-free after seven years and could be IHT-free after two years if you are involved in the farming.

One group of people may escape IHT altogether - where injuries suffered on military service are a contributory factor in a person's death, even after a number of years. This little-known exemption has been of benefit after World War 2 and the Falklands and could apply again post-Iraq and Afghanistan.

ROLES REVERSED

Most advice on saving IHT is based on the assumption that you are the donor and you want to save tax on the assets you leave your family. But the roles may be reversed: you may inherit from an estate which has been hit by IHT because no one did any tax planning or they did it very badly. In that case, you need to consider a .deed of variation.'

Within two years of a person's death, it is possible in effect to re-write their will - so long as all the beneficiaries agree. This can be used to save IHT or to skip a generation, passing assets to grand-children rather than the adult children.

OR YOU JUST EMIGRATE......

This is all too much, you feel, and too complex - so you decide to leave the country. You are looking at changing your domicile, maybe to somewhere such as Italy where there is no IHT. Once you are domiciled abroad, only those assets which are based in the UK will be hit by IHT; while you are domiciled here all of your worldwide assets are subject to IHT. (If you are at all serious about changing your residence or domicile, you will need to access high-quality, very specialist advice)

One definition of domicile is the country which you regard as home, where you intend to be buried. At this point, advisers always tell a tale about Richard Burton, the actor. He lived in Switzerland for a number of years, and people assumed - maybe he did too - that he was domiciled there, and so better off taxwise. But in his will he asked for his coffin to be buried with a Welsh flag. That, it is said, put his domicile straight back into the UK!

****

Chapter 13

Guard What You Own

You have worked hard, you have taken care, built up a nice-sized pile of assets - and there are crooks out there waiting to separate you from what you own. In just one type of scam, identity fraud, Britain has the highest crime rate in Europe. Industry insiders estimate that more than four million Brits have been conned, losing an average £2,000 on a credit card and £7,000 on a bank current account.

Financial crookery is as old as money itself. Take the Spanish prisoner fraud, nowadays called the 419 fraud after the relevant section of the Nigerian criminal code. In this scam, you are asked to provide cash which is needed to free up a large amount of money.(pay a fine to release the prisoner, meet the bill for bank fees, etc, etc) The large amount of money does not exist, and if you do provide cash you will never see it again.

If you give the crook your e-mail address - or he hacks it - he will try a variant. Your friends and family will be contacted and told that you have fallen ill in some distant country. You are short of funds - can they wire some money? If they do, their money will go to an address which the crook controls.

THE CROOK COMES PHISHING

To get at your assets, the crook needs your personal and financial data. So he comes phishing. You get an e-mail which claims to come from a bank or credit card company. Your account, you are told, is going to be frozen unless you confirm your financial data - account numbers, passwords, NI number.

You will be referred to a genuine-looking website which the crook has set up. Once you comply, and provide the data, he is ready to empty your bank account, steal your identity and run up credit card bills.

If you discover you are being phished, resist the temptation to send off a devastating or witty reply. Any response by you is what he is looking for: just log out and check your security.

SPOT A MADOFF

For people who own shares or unit trusts, there is a scary word - Madoff. Just a few years ago, this American financier conned huge amounts of money out of British and American investors. Madoff created the biggest Ponzi scheme of all time - a scam where high dividends are paid out of new purchases made by investors and not out of current earnings.

Madoff sold shares on the back of fake values and performance numbers: his figures were always consistent, which is difficult in the real world and always above average, which is even more difficult. Madoff failed one basic test: if it looks too good to be true, then it probably is.

Canny investors also noticed that Madoff was both a broker and fund manager. This meant that he controlled the shares which investors had bought, so that he could present information including what the shares were worth. A British or American unit trust will place the underlying shares with a bank or other independent trustee.(If you hold unit trusts, check to see who the trustee is)

HYPE AND PROMISES

Hype and grand promises are typically used to fool you into a scam. Another sign of a scam is when you are contacted unexpectedly, by someone you do not know, and asked to give them personal or financial data.

Your bank or credit card company may ask you for this type of data - but only when you contact them!

Beware any deal where time is said to be short and you have to make a quick decision. This is a technique widely used by .boiler rooms' - outfits based outside the UK(so outside British authorities' control) which claim to be brokers and want to sell you shares in a company you have never heard of, but which they tell you will make your fortune. Boiler rooms typically operate by phone.

SNAP DECISION NEEDED

You will have to make a snap decision, there and then or at most 24 hours' time. If you manage to check, you will probably find that the so-called bonanza company does exist - but up-to-date financial data will be hard to find. If you do send money, all you will get is a share certificate of no value.

Just because half of he people in the UK own a computer, defending yourself against fraud depends on computer security. Most computer users buy security software, but a sizeable minority do not - which means running a risk you do not have to take.

When you use a public computer, say in the local library, make sure that you log out and shut down when you have finished your session. Take especial care when you send e-mails and when you access your bank account - some banks will only accept instructions from your own computer.

NETWORKING FOR CROOKS

Many of us use a social networking website, such as Facebook or Myspace, which have become extremely popular in a short time. If you are a user, just reflect how all that personal information will be useful to crooks. Even just your e-mail address is enough to add you to a future phishing scam.

There are some fundamental issues about the net which the crooks can exploit. Probably the most important is that regular e-mail is not secure - which is why big companies and government departments run their own.

If you e-mail your unit trust manager to ask for a valuation, expect to get the details back through the post. Your bank will not accept an important instruction by e-mail, as it may not be able to verify that you were the sender or whether the e-mail was altered.

IDENTITY THEFT

Of all the scams, identity theft is probably the most sinister - when someone steals your personal details and pretends to be you. They steal money from your bank account, spend money on your credit card, take out a loan in your name even apply for a passport. You may only realise that you are a victim when you check your account and card statements or try to get credit. Getting back your identity takes time and means hassle.(It is even possible to insure against the costs of identity theft)

Your identity may have been stolen over the net, but the crooks have other ways. They may go through your rubbish looking for account statements, receipts and credit card slips. They will look for letters and bills which give away your financial information.(Buying a shredder could prove to be one of your best investments)

NEVER GIVE OUT DATA

The crooks may even take the initiative, and write to you or phone you asking for information while pretending to come from a bank or a market research company. The answer is simple: you never give out sensitive data to someone you do not know.

Moving home can be an especially risky time for losing important data. The experts advise you to have mail forwarded by the GPO for at least 12 months after you move. You want to avoid your letters being picked up by the crooks - and you do not know the credit history of the nice man who sold you your new house.

WHAT THE PUBLIC KNOWS

Put yourself in the crook's position - often a good idea in what could be a tricky situation. You will find that a great deal about you is already public knowledge. You can send off for a birth certificate, which will give your date of birth and your mother's maiden name. So when a card company asks for your mother's maiden name as part of their security set-up, make up a name.

You can look up the electoral register and cross-check with the telephone directory to establish the address you are looking for. The

Land Registry will show when you bought your house and how much you paid for it so a tip to the crook that you are well-off and worth scamming. You can look though the director and shareholder list of a listed company and go to a professional register for a doctor, lawyer or accountant.

HOW TO PROTECT YOURSELF

There are a lot of crooks around, and many of them are clever. As well as using common sense, how do you protect yourself? You do not need to live in a bunker, but there are a few sensible steps:

§ Know who you are dealing with. If you are contacted by a company, check with Companies House. If it is a financial operation, contact the Financial Services Authority. You can always go back to the company's own website, but crooks are skilled at setting up a website which looks genuine.

§ Read accounts. Essential that you read - not just glance over - your bank and credit card statements. If there is something you do not recognise, contact the company. Do not just look for big items, as crooks will put small amounts in your card statement to see if you notice. Sometimes there is a simple explanation: the company which takes the money is not the one which sold you the goods.

§ Incoming mail. Be aware of what is being sent to you and when it should arrive - the obvious case is when you order a cheque book from your bank and it fails to turn up, or when a new credit card is overdue.

§ Be wary of unsolicited contacts. Someone may phone or e-mail you telling you that you are due a prize in a lottery that you never entered, that you should buy shares in a far distant oil company etc

etc. Do not take immediate action, try to get names and contact details - and how they got your name in the first place.

§ Be careful with what you do not know. Some people will not use their credit card when they go to an out-of-the-way garage - the attendant might clone the card of someone he has not seen before and may never see again. Best procedure is never let your credit card out of your sight, even in a pub or restaurant.

§ Personal data. Keep these to yourself, above all PIN numbers - if you have been a little careless with your PIN, you may even find that the bank or card company is unwilling to pay compensation. At all times you have to take reasonable care.

§ Credit report. You can get your own credit report from a credit reference agency, and it will cost you only £2. You should check this report every three or six months, and you are entitled to contact the agency in order to correct any errors. You can arrange with the agency for them to e-mail you whenever there is any change to your credit report.

§ Be aware of today's crookery: read the problem letters in newspapers. You will learn, for instance, that in Europe the selling of time share is now controlled, so there has been an expansion of holiday clubs.

****

GLOSSARY

Basis Points: how bankers describe interest rates, with 100 basis points equal to 1%.

BACS: Bankers'
Automated Clearing Service, used to make direct payments from one bank account to another - usually taking three business days.

Bid Price: the (lower)price you get when you shell shares, units or currency.. The difference between the bid price and the (higher)offer price when you buy, represents the spread.

Bonds: fixed-interest, usually fixed-date, debt - company bonds are called(in descending order)investment grade, high yield and junk.

CHAPS: Clearing House Automated Payment System, used to make direct payments from one bank account to another - usually on the same day.

CPI: Consumer Prices Index, used by the Bank of England and increasingly by government - CPI excludes housing costs, and usually rises less fast then RPI.

Credit rating agency: companies, such as Standard & Poor, which publish ratings on countries and companies and on the bonds they issue.

Current Yield/Running Yield: the current level of income from a share or a bond expressed as a percentage of the stock market price.

Default: when a company, or a country, fails to meet the agreed interest and capital repayments which are due on its bonds or other obligations.

Derivatives: assets whose value is fixed by reference to(ie derived from)other assets - options on shares are derivatives.

Distribution Yield: in a unit trust, the amount you could be expected to be paid over the next 12 months.

Due Diligence: going through the books - when a company and its advisers examine a business which it wants to buy.

Gross Redemption Yield: yield applied to bonds, which takes into account any capital profit or loss assuming that the bonds are held to final maturity.

Hedge Funds: often called Absolute Return Funds, which aim to make money whether markets are rising or falling. They typically cover a wide range of assets and use techniques such as short selling.

Historic Yield: dividends paid over the previous 12 months expressed as a percentage of the price.

Identity Theft: when a criminal finds out your personal details and uses these to empty your bank account, buy expensive goods and get credit cards and a passport in your name.

Impaired Life Annuities: annuities which offer a better rate than the average, which are paid to people who smoke, have a history of ill-health or work in strenuous occupations.

LIBOR: London Interbank Offered Rate, the banks' wholesale rate of interest which they charge each other.

Lifestyle Option: moving investments from shares to lower-risk cash or bonds as the beneficiary approaches retirement.

Mark to market: when, e.g. banks, have to show assets at market value - as opposed to what they cost or their own estimate of value.

Monetary Policy Committee: the Bank of England group, including outsiders, which meets every Thursday to fix the level of Base Rate.

Money Laundering: moving money made from crime into the mainstream financial system.

Offer price: the (higher)price you pay when buying shares, units or currency. Also known as the Ask price. The difference between the Offer price and the Bid price is the spread.

Option: an agreement which gives the right, but not the obligation, to buy or sell an asset at a pre-agreed price - you can always walk away from an option.

Ponzi scheme: a financial scam where investors are paid dividends which come not out of income but from capital put up by new subscribers. Bernard Madoff ran the biggest Ponzi scheme ever.(Charles Ponzi was an operator in the US during the 1920s).

Pre-emption rights: the rights of shareholders to approve a large transaction by their company and to buy shares when a public issue is made.

Quantitative Easing: when the Bank of England or the Federal Reserve puts credit into the financial system by buying assets.(Also known as Open Market operations)

Recession: a period when a country's output or income declines for two successive quarters.

Rights issue: when a company raises money by issuing new shares for cash at a discount to the stock market price. The money comes from shareholders, who have the pre-emption rights to subscribe.

RPI: the Retail Prices Index, which is a wide-ranging measure of the cost of living. A rise in RPI=inflation, a fall=deflation.

Securitisation: when debts such as student loans and credit card debt are placed in a company in which shares and bonds can then be sold.

Short selling: when an investor borrows shares to sell, believing that the price will fall so he can then buy them back more cheaply. Short selling of assets is widely used by hedge funds.

Stagflation: when prices are rising faster than the(relatively low) growth in the economy - a problem which caused concern in the UK during 2011.

Stress test: when financial regulators check the likely performance of bank systems against various possible economic situations.

Sub prime: literally .below first class.' Applied to housing loans made to borrowers with a poor financial history.(US term NINJAs - no income, no job, no assets)

SWIFT payment: Society for World-wide Interbank Financial Telecommunications. Used to make a direct payment from a bank account to an overseas account. SWIFT normally takes six working days.

Tiered interest: savings accounts where rates vary depending on the size of your balance. Also used in credit cards, where eg the size of the cashback depends on the amount you spend.

Toxic assets: applied to banks where the assets on which they made loans to customers have dropped in value. Known in the US politely as .Legacy assets.'

Underlying yield: applied to a unit trust, assuming that all the trust's charges and expenses are taken from income.

Warrant: gives the right to buy, usually a share, at a fixed price at a fixed time. Similar to an option, but warrants can be listed separately on the stock market.

Write down: when a company reduces the value at which it shows an asset - to bring it into line with market value, or because circumstances have changed.
Write off: the step which comes after a write down, when a company reduces the value of an asset to zero.

Yield gap: the difference in yield between shares and bonds. When the gap is small, shares may be overvalued; when the gap is large, shares my be cheap.

Useful addresses and websites

Association of Investment Trust Companies (AITC)
Durrant House
8-13 Chiswell Street
London EC1Y 4YY
Hotline: 020 7282 5555
www.aitc.co.uk

Debt Management Office
Eastcheap Court
11 Philpot Lane
London EC3M 8UD
Tel: 0845 357 6500
www.dmo.gov.uk

Department for Work and Pensions (DWP)
If you ring The Pension Service on 0845 606 0265,
You will be connected to the pension centre covering you area,
Or you can look on the website (www.
thepensionservice.gov.uk/contact)

You can obtain DWP leaflets from Pension Service and
Jobcentre Plus office and some post offices, CABs or
Libraries. You can write to:

Pension Guides
Freepost
Bristol BS38 7WA
Tel: 08457 31 32 33
If you have access to the Internet, you can download the leaflets
(and claim forms for many of the benefits)
from www.dwp.gov. uk or www.thepensionservice.gov.uk

Financial Ombudsman
Service (FOS)
South Quay Plaza
183 Marsh Wall
London E14 9SR
Consumer helpline: 0845 080 1800
www.financialombudsman.org.uk

Financial Services Authority (FSA)
25 The North Colonnade
Canary Wharf
London E14 5HS
Consumer helpline: 0845 606 1234
www.fsa.gov.uk/consummer

HM Revenue & Customs (HMRC)
The government department that deals
With al;most all the taxes due in the UK.
Most HMRC leaflets can be obtained
From local tax offices or Tax Enquiry Centres
(look for in the phone book under 'Revenue'
or 'Government Department') or Jobcentre Plus offices.
Almost all are also available on the website at:
www.hmrc.gov.uk or you can ring them the Orderline:
Tel: 0845 900 0404

HM Revenue & Customs National Insurance
Contributions Office (NICO)
Benton Park View
Newcastle upon Tyne NE98 1ZZ
Enquiry Line: 0845 302 1479

International Pension Centre
The Pension Service
Tyneview Park

Newcastle upon Tyne NE98 1BA
Tel: 01912 187777
(8.00am-8.00pm,weekdays)

Investment Management Association
65 Kingsway
London WC2B 6TD
Tel: 020 7831 0898
Information line 020 7269 4639
www.investmentfunds.org.uk
(OEIC.S).

MoneyFACTS
MoneyFacts House
66-70 Thorpe Road
Norwich NR1 1BJ
Tel: 01603 476 178
www.moneyfactsgroup.co.uk

The Pension Service
State Pension Forecasting Team
Future Pension Centre
Tyneview Park
Whitley Road Newcastle upon Tyne NE98 1BA
Tel: 0845 3000 168
www.thepensionservice.gove.uk

Pension Advisory Service
(TPAS)
11 Belgrave Road
London SW1V 1RB
Helpline: 0845 601 2923
www.pensionsadvisoryservice.org.uk

Specialist Magazines
Money Management

3rd Floor
Maple House
149 Tottenham Court Road
London W1P 9LL
020 8606 7545

Planned Savings
6-77 Paul Street
London EC2A 4LG
020 753 1000
Money management and Planned Savings are aimed at professional advisers.

Trade Bodies
The Association of Investment Trust Companies
9th Floor
24 Chiswell Street
London EC1Y 4YY
0207 282 5555
www.itsonline.co.uk www.aitc.co.uk

Provides information on aspects of investing in investment trust companies.

The Investment Management Association
65 Kingsway
London WC2B 6TD
020 7269 4639

www.investmentuk.org
Provides information on investing in unit trusts and Oeics

Proshare
4th Floor Bankside House
107 Leadenhall Street
London EC3A 4AF

0906 802 2222
www.proshare.org.uk

Advises on setting up investment clubs and runs education programmes
for schools on share ownership

The Association of British Insurers
61 Gresham Street
London EC2V 7HQ
020 7600 333
www.abi.org.uk
Publishes information sheets on all aspects of insurance.

The British Insurance Brokers Association
14 Bevis Marks
London EC3A 7NT
0901 814 0015
www.biba.org.uk
www.bsa.org.uk

The Council of Mortgage Lenders
3 Savile Row
London W1S 3BP
020 7437 0655
www.aria.co.uk

Borrowing
The National Debtline
0808 808 4000

The Association of British Credit Unions
Holyoake House
Hanover Street
Manchester M60 OAS
0161 832 8694
www.abcul.org

Credit Information Agencies
Experian
Consumer help services
PO Box 8000
Nottingham NG1 5GX
0870 241 6212
www.experian.com

Equifax Europe (UK)
Credit file advice centre
PO Box 3001
Glasgow G81 0583
0870 010 0583
www.equifax.co.uk

Investment information websites
www.investment-gateway.com
www.new-online-investor.co.uk
www.find.co.uk